To Mike,

Simon

How has the progressive rock band Yes survived 50 years of intense devotion and strong criticism? This book reconsiders the band's musical creativity, variety and value, and highlights an artistic imagination in Yes's finest moments that defies ready-made labels. It illustrates the capacity of honest musical appreciation to remake us, rather than simply to confirm our prejudices.

Simon Barrow is director of the think-tank Ekklesia, and a widely-published writer on politics, beliefs and culture. Music (especially contemporary classical and jazz) has been a major part of his life. He has followed the ebb and flow of Yes music for nearly 45 years.

The author (centre) pictured with the band at Newcastle City Hall in April 2016. L to R: Billy Sherwood (bass), Alan White (drums), Jon Davison (vocals), Geoff Downes (keyboards), Steve Howe (guitars). Photo: Alan Schiff.

The beguiling skill of *Solid Mental Grace* lies in Simon's ability to balance his love for Yes – tested by decades of exposure to their best and worst work – with the incisive and honest skills of a writer with a considerable CV.

This book brings out how the band, ever questing, often fissile, never less than fascinating, have always been more than the sum of their parts.

– Rachel Mann, writing in the Foreword

In memory of Chris Squire, Peter Banks, David Foster, Virgil Howe and Derek Jewell

Chris Squire playing with Yes at Notre Dame University, South Bend, Indiana, USA, 22nd September 1978. Photograph © Kevin Roth

Solid Mental Grace
Listening to the Music of **Yes**

Simon Barrow

Cultured Llama Publishing

Cultured Llama Publishing
INTRA
337–341 High Street
Rochester
ME1 1DA

www.culturedllama.co.uk

Copyright © 2018 Simon Barrow
All rights reserved

Extracts from this material may be copied or passed on to others electronically, provided that the publisher and author approve an e-mail request, the author is fully credited and none of the content is changed

The right of Simon Barrow to be identified as the author of this work has been asserted by him in accordance with Section 77 of the Copyright, Designs and Patents Act 1988

No reproduction of any part of this book may take place, whether stored in a retrieval system, or transmitted in any form, or by any means, electronic, mechanical, photocopying, recording or otherwise, without prior written permission from Cultured Llama Publishing

A CIP record for this book is available from The British Library

This book is sold subject to the conditions that it shall not, by way of trade or otherwise, be lent, re-sold, hired out, or otherwise circulated without the publisher's prior consent in any form of binding or cover other than that in which it is published and without a similar condition including this condition being imposed on the subsequent purchaser

ISBN 978-0-9957381-8-8

Printed in Great Britain by Lightning Source UK Ltd

Cover design: Mark Holihan

Cover image: Utah, 21st November 2010. 'Heart of the Sunrise', © Jonathan Crawford

Foreword: © Rachel Mann

Foreword

For a critic, 'love' is a dangerous virtue. It implies a partiality that might get in the way of sound analysis. Arguably, a critic – at their best – never wants to lose sight of truth, quality and cool judgment. As a music critic, I always want to hold the work I write about to the very highest standards.

Yet, love matters. It's what drives us to become critics and music journalists in the first place. In short, we begin as fans. *Solid Mental Grace,* Simon Barrow's new book about listening to the music of Yes, is profoundly grounded in passion. He knows the power of first musical love – that visceral encounter with a band or artist that changes the way we experience the world.

For him, it was hearing *Tales From Topographic Oceans'* expansive and mystical movements back in 1974 that opened a path which has led him back and forth through Yes's timeline. It has generated a fascination akin to faith. Definitely not blind faith, I hasten to add. The beguiling skill of *Solid Mental Grace* lies in Simon's ability to balance his love for Yes – tested by decades of exposure to their best and worst work – with the incisive and honest skills of a writer with a considerable CV.

At a point when so many of progressive rock's heroes, including Chris Squire and Peter Banks, have gone to the great gig in the sky, it is surely time for a reappraisal of Yes on the scale the author conceives. Yes remain a definitive band whose influence, not least on contemporary giants like Steven Wilson, is beyond question.

This book brings out how the band, ever questing, often fissile, never less than fascinating, have always been more than the sum of their parts. By daring to travel 'close to the edge',

Simon Barrow reveals Yes's power to take the listener to 'the gates of delirium'.

– Rachel Mann, March 2018

Rachel Mann writes about progressive music, metal and folk for *Prog* magazine, *The Quietus* and *AltSounds,* among others. She is an author, musician, priest and feminist/queer philosopher and theologian. From 2009 – 2017 Rachel was Poet in Residence at Manchester Cathedral. Her books include *Fierce Imaginings* (2017) and *Dazzling Darkness* (2012).

Contents

Foreword	vii
Introduction	1
1 Overture: Sound Chaser	5
2 In the Beginning is the Future (*1968-1969*)	19
3 Wake Up and Dream (*1970-1972*)	31
4 Seasons Will Pass You By (*Close to the Edge*)	47
5 High the Memory (*Tales From Topographic Oceans*)	63
6 Electric Freedom (*Relayer*)	83
7 Here We Can Be (*Going for the One*)	95
8 Forward Out This Feeling (*1978-1991*)	107
9 Speaking New Languages (*1991-1997*)	121
10 Turn Around and Remember (*1998-2004*)	137
11 Along the Edge (*2005-2011*)	151
12 Second Attention (*2012-2018 and beyond*)	165
13 Passions That Flow (*Yes Live*)	175
14 Yes After 'Progressive Rock' (*50 years and onwards*)	183
15 Coda: Total Yes Retain?	195
Acknowledgements	201
About the Author	202
Appendix I: Discography	203
Appendix II: Bibliography	208
Appendix III: Yes Classics	214
Appendix IV: Further Resources	218

Introduction

Only connect the prose and the passion, and both will be exalted... Live in fragments no longer.

– E. M. Forster

Connect indeed, and, for musical purposes, *listen*. Open your ears to passionate possibilities, awkward challenges and surprising invitations. In so doing, dare to say 'yes' – not naïvely, recklessly or to repress failings and questions, but because discerning what to affirm is the essence of living in the midst of life's disappointments and failings. It is also a vital part of appreciating music beyond its surface impressions or the noisy claims of the 'business' that often engulfs it.

Something of that spirit of openness and expectation is intended to imbue this book, with its (to some) curious subject: the music of progressive rock doyens, Yes. The enterprising publisher, Cultured Llama, which is pleasingly broad in its literary range, bravely took on this particular title as one of a growing catalogue of non-fiction books under the appropriate rubric 'Curious Things'. The music of Yes is nothing if not curious, though ironically its treatment by journalists and pundits has often failed to evidence much actual curiosity. Musical pigeonholes and assumptions, such as those sometimes purveyed by *Rolling Stone* magazine, have instead predominated. The genuine, worthy musical affirmation that I suggest can legitimately be discovered at the heart of Yes's recorded output over some fifty years has too easily been bypassed in a welter of lazy dismissal. The purpose of this book is not so much to 'set the record straight' (that would be unhelpfully moralistic) as it is to offer, knowingly but unapologetically, another perspective: one that aims to be serious without being po-faced, and thoughtful without being indigestible. No doubt I will, like my subjects, fall short at some points. But I hope the journey will prove enlivening, nonetheless.

As the introductory 'Overture' Chapter notes, the title of this book, *Solid Mental Grace*, is a line from what many – including some of the band's great army of critics – regard as their greatest single achievement, the 1972 album *Close to the Edge*. For me, these three words pose a couple of helpful questions. Can that which is essentially solid and earthbound allow itself to be transformed by openness to what we might call transcendence? Equally, is something that evokes the noetic plane capable of remaining substantial, rooted, communicable? Music that truly captivates and endures suggests that it is. Exploring the shape and form that music takes is another way of testing both hypotheses, thereby gaining greater appreciation of what lies in or between the notes.

That is also the reason for my sub-title. This is not intended to be another biography or hagiography of Yes. Instead, it is about what happens when we listen, learning to listen afresh, and the fruits of listening. It takes as its task a sympathetic but nevertheless critically aware appraisal of the music the band has composed, arranged, produced and performed over – remarkably enough – part of six decades (yup, do the maths). Insofar as there is a 'Yes story' to be told, I am interested in trying to find out what it would be like for the music to narrate that story, and those who people it, rather than the other way round. The reader can judge whether this is finally feasible or not. It means that, somewhere within these pages, you will find an account of almost every recorded piece of music Yes has generated – many great, some craftsman like, a number falling short (on the measurements I value, anyway), as with all human enterprises. The glory is in the flaws, too; and vice versa. There are also individual chapters on the live experience of the band, the perilousness of labelling music, and the question of legacy.

As for the book's perspective, it is, as I unpack in the introductory Chapter, that of someone 'lost in music' of great variety, and over many years, but first schooled by the disciplines of the classical tradition. That has its own weaknesses and biases, of course. I try to acknowledge those, and to offer judgements that are reserved as well as engaged, distinguishing wherever possible personal preferences from judgements about quality, and trying to hear the different styles and forms of music Yes have attempted over the years in some kind of appropriate context. Reflecting on the subjective and objective experience of listening to music generally is part of what is attempted herein, as well as close attention to one particular collection of music.

To aid the reader and listener, I have included CD track times in minutes and seconds (e.g. 20:20) to quite a few of my comments on Yes's *oeuvre*. Although there are a few technical remarks about the music, this book is not offered as a piece of music theory – which is, in any case, not my primary area of competence. What I have tried to do instead is to paint a picture of sound in words, but with some anticipation that the reader might choose to pay attention to the actual recorded notes, and certainly to give them priority over any of my authorial flights of fancy. Words are signposts; music is the signifier. You can't write about music much better than you can dance about architecture, perhaps. But you *can* throw some ink, thoughts and limbs around to see if they help make a meaningful shape of what is being referred to!

There are one or two surprises for the author as well as the reader in the pages that follow. Some Chapters are quite a bit longer than others. That is a matter of selection and emphasis. Equally, I found myself devoting more attention to 2011's *Fly From Here* than many might feel it merits, for example. But that is because it highlights some of the band's less familiar work in its later years. On the other hand, I have not devoted much space to the 'extras' and demos included in many recent Yes re-releases, or to the voluminous number of live bootlegs. The later albums are generally given less space. So *Solid Mental Grace* is shorter and less detailed than it started out intending to be. Because research and reflective writing has been a solid part of my professional life for many years, it was tempting to write a lengthily footnoted 'treatise' on Yes. Indeed, that's how it began, way back in 2009. Thankfully I was dissuaded from that path, though a bit of the denser writing may emerge in web material associated with a book that I hope you will find pleasingly, and perhaps unexpectedly, short. In the end my solution to the quandary of over-thinking was to end up writing what you hold in your hands in an alarmingly short period of time. Sometimes, in life and music, spontaneity is a necessary gift.

Lastly, I should stress that, while I think the alleged genre of 'progressive rock' (about which I remain something of a deliberate agnostic) is often unfairly traduced in an ignorantly generalising way, I am no particular defender of 'prog' as some kind of whole. Indeed I'm still not sure whether it really exists. See Chapter 14 for evidence. As for Yes music, I do not aspire to defend that either, though I cannot help loving it, and if I did not think it was eminently worthy of attention I simply would not bother writing about it. So in the final analysis I am an advocate. Of course. But hopefully not a tone deaf one.

Those caveats and guidelines aside, enjoy what follows. But, far better, enjoy the glorious musical journey it seeks to evoke: Yes – beyond, between and before. For as E. M. Forster also wrote, both as an invitation and a warning: "Romance only dies with life. No pair of pincers will ever pull it out of us."

– Simon Barrow, March 2018

Chapter 1
Overture:
Sound Chaser

Listening to the music of Yes is like listening to the wind and the sea and the sunlight and the humming core of the planet all at once: it is unity, it is totality. It is the sound of affirmation. It is the sound of life. And to life you can say only 'yes'.

– Dan Hedges

In the case of Yes, [an] often overbearing pretentiousness resulted in moments of rare grace and beauty, a bizarre and fleeting – if totally unrealistic – coupling of classical textures with rock pathos.

– Ernesto Lechner

It all began in the autumn of 1974, during a series of late night listening sessions in an artificially darkened room. In those treasured moments a strange love affair with the music of Yes was born. Little did I know that, some 44 years later, the fatal attraction would still be there: older, wiser and considerably more questioning, but just as capable of feeling and generating genuine passion. Once the muse has bitten, there is no getting away from it. So this book is, in no small part, an attempt to find out what forces are at work when such an odd musical magnetism casts its spell upon us.

A band revered for a season several decades ago, nowadays

Yes are more likely to be casually reviled or ignored by all but their aficionados – of whom there still remain a surprising number. My aim here is to re-examine the band's output over fifty years and to offer a critical appreciation of its significance; something many would still regard as dangerous or forbidden territory, given the extremes of adulation and opprobrium the band has often attracted.

Upon examination, it is noticeable that contemporary commentators who refer to Yes, often simply to write them off, rarely pay any serious attention to their actual music. Among a majority of critics, Yes have become a vague but inflated cipher for a certain kind of cultural unacceptability – one that arguably has more to do with fashion's poisoned expectations than with any particular attempt at understanding. What has fed the routine dismissals is most often a raw assertion of the primacy of the visceral and the 'cool' in rock subcultures. Something that brooks little reasoned argument. Equally, it must be acknowledged that there is indeed plenty to deride in the cultural milieu that Yes have been taken to occupy centre-stage. The bizarre costumes, stage theatrics, quirky indulgences and soap opera-like personnel sagas, for a start.

Nevertheless, as far as I am concerned, it is the *music* that Yes have produced, at its very best "finely wrought, delicate, sophisticated and drawing on a host of influences" (Derek Jewell, writing in the liner notes for volume three of the UK *Sunday Times* 1975 triple LP, *The Rock Revelation*) which truly matters, rather than (say) the often told stories of their interpersonal upheavals or the alleged role they played in foisting a sonic crime lazily dubbed 'progressive rock' onto a hoodwinked generation.

Not that this simplifies things. Because, to anyone who has given it more than a cursory hearing, 'Yes music' turns out to be a decidedly unpredictable beast. Neither pure stock nor obvious hybrid in the sound universe it most obviously inhabits, it employs deceptively familiar forms to evoke what in its most sublime moments is an almost otherworldly aesthetic. Yet it rarely conforms to the quick summaries of those who are instantly dismissive or overly devotional.

For example, Yes's work is not in any substantive sense 'symphonic'. Nor is it gratuitously virtuosic, culpably neglectful of the idioms that birthed it, needlessly complex, nor meandering and shapeless. A little analysis can readily demonstrate these points. That people frequently say things like this about it illustrates rather vividly how our relationship with music is (of course) as much about our own feelings, failings and foibles as it is about those curious objects of desire – the assembled notes themselves. Yet there remains no simple way to extricate one from the other. The subjective and projective elements in all music criticism and appreciation have to be accepted rather than fought against. This does not mean that meaningful judgements cannot be offered, discussed, sustained and disputed. But it does imply that personal (and social, cultural) history and affection play more than a small role in reaching those positions. In this respect, my background is probably a little unusual for someone writing about a rock band. Some back-story may therefore be needed to explain how and why I come at 'things Yes'.

Unbeknown to him, the person who afforded my formal introduction to the band in that candle-lit room was the late *Sunday Times* jazz correspondent Derek Jewell, whose warmly discursive style (imagine doyen broadcaster Alistair Cook with a very large record collection) guided some of BBC Radio Three's earlier explorations into what was, for them, the comparatively uncharted territory of 'popular music'. His weekend review programme, featuring commentary and interviews interweaved with a wide-ranging selection of music, was simply entitled 'Sounds Interesting'. That describes precisely what it aimed to do: to entice, illuminate and inform.

Most definitely an 'old school' music writer and broadcaster, Jewell reserved his harsher judgements for private conversation and proffered a public discourse that remained consistently polite, enthusiastic and thoughtful – flowerily reverential even, at times. Managing to draw in a broad listenership without intending to patronise or dumb down, he was disarmingly serious in his mission to use the archetypal classical music station for unveiling delights as varied as Joni Mitchell, Soft Machine, Nina Simone, Jaco Pastorius, Joan Armatrading, Duke Ellington and Brand X. Yes came to be among his several favourites.

Derek Jewell's encouraging voice was to me the gateway into an alternative musical storehouse where virtue, preservation and worth was still determined by rich appreciation and devotion, rather today's ironic detachment. Such an approach will seem unforgivably earnest to most contemporary audiences. But for me, reared in a household where Bach, Beethoven, Mozart, Haydn, Brahms, Mendelssohn, Schumann and Schubert ruled the roost ('background music' was not readily practised!), it became a pathway to new pastures in sound by means of a vehicle I understood in terms of a received classical frame – one built on awe, curiosity and attentiveness, rather than the commercial bright lights thrown out by DJs bearing jingles.

The remembering
Perhaps it is hard to think of a child formed in the late '60s and early '70s who could grow up largely disconnected from the musical culture that was shaking the foundations of his generation: one epitomised by Lennon, Jagger, Hendrix and the Velvet Underground. But that was, to a large extent, me. I started out as a thoroughgoing, slightly old-fashioned 'classical kid', though with a nascent sense of adventure. Sure, I soon enjoyed a surface flirtation with Petula Clark's uplifting show tunes, with the blurring notes of Georgie Fame and the Blue Flames

(whose true merits I came to appreciate only years later), and then with the gloriously illicit, sax-inflected sleaze of Bowie's 'Drive-In Saturday'. But beyond a few guilty pleasures, Argo shaped my earliest listening habits much more than Apple. Well, composer John Tavener's *The Whale* aside. For someone from my social and cultural background that was how it was 'supposed to be'. Respect meant respectability. Then, thankfully, tough new questions and exciting possibilities began to shake all those forgone conclusions about music.

The first piece of vinyl I truly fell for, in the full-blown sense that leaves you overwhelmingly 'lost in music', turned out to be Karl Richter's 1960s recording of Handel's Organ Concertos, opus 7, numbers 9–12, diligently performed with the soloist's own Chamber Orchestra. It didn't exactly make me an instant hit with the girls, but it provided the listening foundations for a lifetime's musical journeying. My gratitude to David Allen, the family friend who gifted me that unexpectedly seductive LP, is beyond calculation. Indeed, within eighteen months, I had played my way through that disc so often that I had to replace it out of my rather modest pocket money because it had begun to wear away with use. Also, the original was Decca mono, while the replacement edition was stereo.

Then in 1972, on the cusp of turning fourteen, I ventured into a music store in Eastbourne. The night before, I had been required to sit through several Beethoven late string quartets (which intrigued me no end), a symphony and, incongruously, two sides of Shirley Bassey (which I found less than enthralling at the time). At the behest of my parents' good friends, Brian and Margaret Hodgson, who lived on the south coast, these 'music and supper' evenings took place every few months – to complement our own domestic ones. I often experienced a sense of youthful rebellion against what was chosen for my aural edification. But I was incorrigibly polite in those days, and the discipline of being made to concentrate, even against your initial instincts, was one I came to value enormously. Besides, that record store outing on a bright, sunny morning turned out to be a date with destiny.

For some inexplicable reason, as I walked into the shop, my eyes lit upon a recording of Bartók's second violin concerto. It was the cover, all bold brush strokes and in-your-face modernism, which initially won me over. Concerning the music, my parents confidently informed me: 'You'll hate it'. What more motivation could a 13-year-old need? I passed my money across the counter, rushed home, pressed the disc onto my record deck and began to listen with a growing sense of bemusement and distress. My parents were right, it seemed. To my rather untutored ears, Bartók in his confrontational prime sounded cacophonous, incoherent ... but also peculiarly intriguing. Even more so than those remarkable late Beethoven quartets. Unwilling to be defeated, I told them Bartók was 'interesting' and proceeded to play the recording again and again, probably fifteen or sixteen times over the course of several nights, until my head began to acclimatise to a sound world that was drivingly rhythmic, angular, elusive, discordant, and melodic in a way that I had not tasted before, and yet also startlingly tender.

What I learned from this early episode was that much of the music which will stay with you for good – including music that can touch your soul, your intellect and your feet all at the same time – takes hard work and an open mind. Lasting value rarely reveals itself on first acquaintance. From that point on, I never looked back. Ravel, Stravinsky, Shostakovich, Kodály, Britten, Poulenc and many more found their way onto my turntable, to be followed in future times by everything from Ornette Coleman to Olivier Messiaen, from Miles Davis to Michael Tippett, from Godspeed You! Black Emperor to Harrison Birtwistle. Gradually I began to fill in the rather gaping holes in my autodidactic musical education. Late night Radio Three became a sanctuary for me in my formative listening years. John Peel too, when I needed something completely uncharted. The classical frame was still writ large, though. So while the family watched television of an evening, I would retire to my room, turn on the radio, switch off the lights, and immerse myself in exhilarating musical climes I had not experienced before. Which is how I discovered Yes, via Derek Jewell's ministrations.

Friends at college had already begun to push me to take at least a passing interest in this now questionable thing called 'progressive rock'. Emerson, Lake and Palmer's first album (conceived before the really corrosive bombast set in) was among the first that I borrowed, on account of its Bartók-connected opener, 'The Barbarian', propelled forward by stabs of Hammond-driven dissonance. 'The Three Fates' organ and piano suite also drew me in, along with a wonderful Oscar Petersen-influenced interlude on 'Take a Pebble'. I was hooked. But I had no idea what else to listen to, until I was introduced to a new programme when Keith Emerson's now familiar version of the Allegro Barbaro jumped unexpectedly out at me from the radio one evening.

That was how I locked into Jewell's 'Sounds Interesting', which abruptly acquainted me with John McLaughlin and the Mahavishnu Orchestra. The trailer also told me that, the following week, the broadcast would revolve around the 22-minute opening piece on Yes's upcoming album *Relayer*. Still struggling to imagine how a rock band could articulate itself convincingly over more than a handful of bars (other than by aping the classics), I tuned in and found myself swept away. Not that I instantly warmed to 'The Gates of Delirium', with its steely fusion of lyricism and apocalypse. But there was something quite special there, I could tell. It tantalised me. I wanted to hear and learn more. It drew me in.

The first move after that was headlong back into 1973's *Tales From Topographic Oceans*, four expansive (but still strangely coherent) pieces of music inspired by offbeat commentary on some Hindu shastras, clocking in at a little under 80 minutes in total. Given that much of the classical repertoire I absorbed regularly spanned an hour or so, the length didn't take me aback. Emboldened, I launched into those fateful late-night listening sessions in order to really get my head (and heart) around this pleasingly strange music. Only later did I discover that many rock critics had a fetish for three-minute wonders, and cast grave suspicion, if not contempt, on anyone who tried to extend the genre's vocabulary too far – sometimes with justification, but on other occasions in an unnecessarily reductionist way.

Topographic came across to me as music rooted in rock, though not so much in blues, heading off to explore a range of cultures, textures and dynamics. It was an odd, uninhibited and compelling concoction; exactly the sort of thing I had been searching for, without quite knowing it. By contrast, the previous album, *Close To The Edge,* from 1972, sounded almost reassuring, combining rhythmic inventiveness and harmony with a sense of expectant grandeur that was panoramic in its vision, delicacy and intensity. Then I returned to *Relayer* once more, this time with a surer sense of the landscape on which the musicians were operating.

So this is how Yes's music made its impact on me – as something fresh, thoughtful, exciting, stirring, challenging and powerfully emotional. I have no doubt that Dan Hedges' paean (the opening quote of this Chapter, from the 1975 UK tour programme) sounds laughably overblown in a cynical era and with the hindsight of 44 years. But it spells out exactly how I felt when I heard Yes live for the first time in 1977. The music cut straight to the heart without bypassing the head or leaving the body unmoved. It was enticingly 'cosmic' and deeply personal all in one inviting sweep. No additional hallucinogenic was required!

My points of entry into the band's muse had been, as it turned out, the three albums that, for many who appreciate what has come to be called the 'classic Yes' sound, define the band at the pinnacle of its powers. At the same time, for the group's legion detractors, shaped by a school of criticism epitomised by Lester Bangs and *Rolling Stone* magazine, *Tales*, in particular, embodies everything wrong with art rock – music that is seen as over-inflated, self-conscious, endlessly elaborated, and underneath all that essentially vapid: "much sound and fury, signifying nothing".

These are not baseless complaints. Like its close cousin, jazz-rock fusion, 'prog' has inflicted more than its fair share of note-filled emptiness and baroque bad taste on the world. But these days its failings are assumed well ahead of any actual attempt to get to grips with the huge variety of music, some of it of considerable quality, subsumed under that moniker. For even good journalists, like Ernesto Lechner (again quoted above) it has become necessary to disguise underlying admiration with almost ritualistic references to "overbearing pretentiousness". This is a shame. In the case of Yes, it risks marginalising some tremendous creative achievements. On the other hand, without a genuine sense of the vulnerability and flaws of the musicians involved, both individually and collectively, you would end up with little more than a dubious *apologia* – fandom plus footnotes.

So while I have no wish to deny strong affection for, and affiliation to, the music of Yes (I would hardly bother to write if this was not the case), my purpose is neither to defend the indefensible, nor to cajole the unwilling into grudging acceptance. Rather, it is to offer a friendly but not uncritical invitation to musical appreciation – in much the same way that Derek Jewell used to. "Give this a go, listen afresh, gain some perspective, allow yourself the possibility of surprise, and then see what transpires." That applies equally to those coming fresh to Yes's music, and to those whose palate has been conditioned, angled or jaded by previous encounters. Real listening always enables some element of 'beginning afresh', even in the midst of familiarity – actual or presumed.

Waiting to feel the sound

It is my experience that music really can be fruitfully enhanced, enlivened and 'situated' by critical appreciation: that is, by the attempt to understand and value it on something like its own terms, without either imposing too much prefiguring ideology, or shirking the duty to face its particular demands and limits. For this to happen, however, music has to be properly *heard* – especially in a world where everything that frames it (the hype, the presentation, the speculation, the industry) detracts so readily from what the ear may discover and learn. The art of listening is something that has elicited theory by the jarful, too. Being a theoretician in other areas, I am not dismissive or disrespectful of that. But you do not need to be a theorist to hear meaningfully. You need to be someone capable of having your ears opened, discerning something different, relating it to what has already been received, and exploring its impact on yourself and others as 'listening subjects' – persons upon whom music can in some sense write its own agenda so that it becomes part of their own.

That, I guess, is what Yes's music has done with me. Much of the time these days I hear it not as something 'out there', but as part and parcel of an internal dialogue, replete with joys and concerns, doubts and reassurances. That does not mean, however, that I have become incapable of standing beyond its thrall, of examining and exploring it from an evaluative distance. What I am seeking in this book is something of a conversation between these two – the interlocking interpretative horizons of passionate engagement and honestly reflective detachment. In reality, one depends upon the other. You cannot be trusted to account for a world you have not properly engaged with; but also you cannot truly discover something new if you have not stood at its threshold with a sense of both anticipation and reservation.

"Most of all, play with the game of the age", sings Jon Anderson on 1978's 'Madrigal'. Like all worthwhile artistic enterprises, Yes's music exists both inside and outside the era that most decisively shaped it, the 1970s – a time of dazzle, dreaming and disco, but also of eager exploration rooted in the aspirations of the 1960s and tempered by the gradual implosion of that decade's less realisable hopes. This was the uncertain space in which Yes emerged. They evolved, wrote publicist Dan Hedges, "from writing simple 32 bar songs to creating complete, complex works ... The whole group [has become] a single dazzling mind. Instruments and voices are employed as an orchestra and choir, weaving a tapestry of sound that is overwhelming in its final impact."

Within a few short years, the band had leapt unexpectedly from riffing with 'In the Midnight Hour' and covering Leonard Bernstein's 'Something's Coming' to creating albums of audacious, suite-like ambition. Whether we fully enjoy the results or not, it is unfair to call this shift 'pretension'. There was little artifice here; more a burning desire to push musical boundaries at a time when studios and record producers offered what today looks like unimaginable artistic freedom. Yes were simply doing what any group of young, aspiring, capable musicians might choose in similar circumstances, aided by the reckless abandon of the times, youthful *naïveté* perhaps, the lure of growing fame, and the presence of audiences keen to see how the energy of rock could be combined with a range of other musical influences made suddenly accessible by what turned out to be the first airwaves of globalisation.

The game of the age
According to the standard narrative, it was the brutalities of punk and new wave that brought this whole edifice crashing

down, humbling an art form that had moved away from the people and into the hands of unaccountable, elite musicians and producers. In fact, progressive rock and punk co-existed for several years, each continuing to draw sizeable audiences. There was even some overlap. It was more the blandishments of commercial radio and the depressing rise of bland, format-friendly AOR (Adult/Album-Oriented Rock) that truly destroyed the art rock enterprise, further seducing young men with celebrity and dollars. Groups like Genesis and ELP morphed into glorified pop-rock outfits. Yes, to some extent, both followed and bucked that trend. In different ways, 1980's *Drama* and the surprise 1984 re-launch *90125*, even if they were many fathoms away from those *Topographic Oceans*, adapted to the sensibilities of the moment while containing distinct echoes and reworking of past glories – on the former album *Drama*, particularly, which in the wake of the band's fiftieth anniversary has become almost a 'standard'.

But since those dwindling guitar harmonics that brought the magnificent 'Awaken' to a close, some would still say that the group has never really recovered the unalloyed spirit of their "solid time of change", 1971–1977. As Lechner truthfully observes in his 2004 biographical note for *The New Rolling Stone Album Guide*:

> Since 1996, [Jon] Anderson and a revolving cast of former and new members have attempted a return to the classically influenced Yes sound of yesteryear. Truth be said, there are bits and pieces of the old magic to be found in the underwhelming *The Ladder* and the orchestrally enhanced *Magnification*. For the most part, however, Yes has left its maddening grandeur behind.

Well, almost. After the longest hiatus in their uneven history, Yes intended to return to the arenas and concert halls again in 2008, revisiting the music that truly distinguished them, reprising more recent work, and throwing in one or two surprises.

That ended up being postponed until 2009 and onwards. Whether a fitting *dénouement* is possible remains to be seen. But I suspect future generations will recognise more of what they truly achieved in their prime than seems remotely possible right now. In any event, the aftermath of the band's elevation to the commercially flatulent 'Rock'n'Roll Hall of Fame' (2016) and the fiftieth anniversary of their formation (2018), seems as good a time as any to rekindle the Yes spirit and to ask what kind of legacy it leaves, other than as a nostalgic distraction for those of us with a hunger first stoked in the shadowy rooms of our earlier musical imagination.

The title of this book, as anyone familiar with Yes will know, is one of many curiously concocted phrases thrown out by the Hermann Hesse inspired *Close To The Edge*. There is, it seems to me, an abiding 'solid mental grace' in Yes's music; a kind of longing for fulfilment that is both substantial and elusive, curiously powerful and yet very fragile. My principal musical interests these days are in very different spheres, but somehow the Yes flame continues to flicker, attract and illuminate in the background.

Meanwhile, if any of these musings, ordered in generally chronological sequence, but seeking connections in many directions, assist somebody in discovering what is of abiding value in Yes's finest music, I will of course be pleased. However, my reason for writing is not primarily advocacy, but understanding. It is also essentially the same as my reason for continuing to listen to Yes; because, inexplicably but joyously, I find that I have to.

Chapter 2
In the Beginning is the Future (1968–1969)

> We are the music makers, and we are the dreamers of dreams.
> — Arthur O'Shaughnessy

Unlike those other progenitors of post-1967 experimental rock, King Crimson, Yes did not give the impression of having sprung fully-formed from a mature musical womb. When they first made their appearances on stage in 1968 and then on disc the following year, most of them had a history in other short-lived musical outfits. Compared with many of their contemporaries on the music scene they shone with confidence, invention and accomplishment. But there were rough edges, moments of uncertainty, lack of experience and uneven musical surfaces on display, too.

With hindsight, the band's initial recorded offerings, *Yes* and *Time and a Word,* turned out to be invitational, transitional affairs – albeit with more than enough tokens, signals and premonitions of the glories to come during the band's defining period – from 1971's *The Yes Album* through to *Relayer* in 1974, and then in the final flourish of that classic era with 'Awaken' on 1977's *Going for the One*. Neither of those 'launch' recordings lack moments of genuine musical quality. But in the light of what was to come, perhaps they do fall short on the compositional coherence, the performative finesse and (above all) the production artistry that would subsequently become hallmarks of the group's development in their '70s heydays and beyond. Even so, there is enough substance in the debut LP and its successor to provide clear foundations for the quantum leap that followed the arrival of groundbreaking new guitarist Steve Howe in April 1970, and which quickly led to the release of the band's all-important third disc, *The Yes Album*, on 29 January 1971.

Something's definitely coming

The eponymous first album, *Yes*, was recorded in early 1969. It appeared as an LP in Britain on 25 July 1969, and subsequently debuted in Holland and Germany at the end of August, in North America on 15 October, and thence in Japan, Italy and other parts of Europe. Its curious character – part ballad, part rock, part music-hall and part psychedelia, with occasional echoes of experimentalism – was shaped by several factors: the intriguing diversity of that first band line-up; an unsettling array of musical directions inherent in the kaleidoscopic culture of the late sixties; the practical instability of early Yes's existence, and the young musicians' struggle to master studio techniques adequately to convey the fresh musical ideas they were coming up with. In short, the 'project', if you can call it that, hinged awkwardly on the attempt to bridge an as-yet-unnameable gap between the music cascading around the band's collective mind and the resources needed to realise something so sprawling and organic in the essentially static medium of primitive vinyl.

In his enthusiastic but informed 2010 overview of progressive rock, music journalist Will Romano quotes multi-instrumentalist Ian McDonald as suggesting that, in spite of the divergent personalities in the band, "[t]he original King Crimson agreed on more or less everything [in] musical terms ... We were all in the same place." It would be very hard to say that of Yes. Indeed, according to drummer Bill Bruford, "Yes only ever disagreed." That was due, in no small part, to the rather different cultures from which the initial members all came, both temperamentally and musically (and to a significant extent socially, too). Co-founder Jon Anderson was a nightclub-style singer with an alto range, a working-class, northern English background, and the restless mental and spiritual curiosity of an autodidact. Bassist Chris Squire, on the other hand, with whom Anderson forged the alliance that essentially created Yes, had lived in suburban north London, brushed up against a minor public school, and had been immersed in English church music alongside '60s pop from an early age. Their point of contact, negotiated across a significant cultural and physical gulf, with the giant instrumentalist towering over the petite singer, was a mutual love of layered vocal harmonies deployed by the likes of Simon and Garfunkel, the Byrds, the Beatles and The Association.

Next into the mix came Bill Bruford, a sharply intelligent drummer with an instinctive love of jazz, a handful of percussion lessons, a bit of peer tutoring, and some subsequent contrary inclinations towards a degree in economics at the University of Leeds. He was ambitious, talented and practical. The only one who noted receipts while on tour. Guitarist Peter Banks, on the other hand, was an eclectic, self-activating rock guitarist with a turbulent spirit, and organist Tony Kaye was a slick Hammond M-100 player and art school dropout with a smattering of classical training. None of them could have been described as 'easy' types, and all wanted to pull in ambitious directions, without being particularly sure about where they might end up. Yet there was also what seemed to be a shared exploratory synergy, a sense that the world was ready for more than three-minute pop wonders, a desire to sound new and interesting, youthful hubris, and a flowering artistic imagination arising from the exhilarating freedom provided by the post-*Sergeant Pepper* London landscape.

To those with aspirations and technical prowess, anything seemed possible at the time. That said, early Yes gigs, starting at the Rachel McMillan College, featured mostly covers. These included almost free-form versions of tunes like Wilson Pickett's 'In the Midnight Hour', and increasingly patterned, angular takes on Leonard Bernstein and Stephen Sondheim's 'Something's Coming', from the iconic *West Side Story*, to which we will return. Then Banks and Bruford saw King Crimson in action and realised that there was another level. Yes needed to rehearse better, experiment creatively and explore widely. They were all up for the challenge, but uncertain as to how to proceed.

By the time those initial recording sessions for what was to become *Yes* took place, amidst gigging and hustling, there was probably a greater musical foment taking place within the group than the final recorded product shows forth. This was partly because of the band's relative lack of experience in the studio, lack of time (the whole process was ludicrously short compared to some of the subsequent, overblown, adventures) and the somewhat stilted approach of producer Paul Colton – who was not used to the more edgy style of these young pretenders. The resulting LP did not set the world on fire in commercial terms, but it nevertheless began to attract the attention of a small coterie of seasoned journalists and industry listeners who would later play an important role in projecting Yes towards a wider and more appreciative audience. They included Tony Wilson in *Melody Maker*, whose assessment was subsequently included as a liner note in the album. "There was life, vitality and musicianship in their approach," he wrote. "They have a superior vocal sound – assured, clear and harmonic. They knew what they were doing and they did it with style. It showed in their own songs and imaginative arrangements."

Rediscovering the past
In listening to *Yes,* a useful contrast is provided by attending both to the original 1969 LP and the later CD release, and then comparing these with the 2003 Rhino re-mastered CD, which also includes six bonus tracks – including two versions of 'Something's Coming', which did not make the album, together with other material that prefigured *Time and a Word*. Evidently, the latter has far more detail and depth, though the limitations of the source tapes impose real constraints on what can be discerned. As with all the other albums explored in this book, my own comments arise from long-term listening, but also from a conscious decision to stand back and approach the material 'as new', insofar as one can. Taking a break does, despite the loss of innocence inevitably involved in underlying familiarity, provide fresh perspective and generate some interesting surprises – even many years on.

In fact, my initial aural encounter with the album *Yes* took place a full nine years after it was recorded. It was not until 1978 that I first listened both to this original LP and to *Time and a Word*. By that time, Yes had for me peaked musically with 'Awaken' on *Going for the One,* and looked as if they would be in sharp, or perhaps terminal, decline following the energetic but patchy *Tormato*. Also by that time, my own listening habits had been strongly shaped by the three extensive musical summits laid out on *Close to the Edge* (1972), *Tales From Topographic Oceans* (1973) and *Relayer* (1974). So this was the comparatively complex, evolved sonic world that provided my horizons in approaching the original foothills of Mount Yes. What inspired me to do so was what you could call nostalgia for a different future. *Tormato* had felt like a dramatic descent from the 1970s heights, in spite of its several inspiring moments. (I was later to hear it differently, but that's how it appeared at the time.) So would revisiting the 'early years' provide some fresh resources for appreciating where the band had emerged from and where it might be going – if anywhere? Or to put it more sanguinely, could the roots of the 'classic' period provide consolation for passed (let alone past) glories? What had I been missing out on for the past nine years – which at that time seemed an aeon in rock history?

Personally speaking, there was precedent for seeking fresh fruit from a reverse-listening journey. In between *Relayer* and *Going for the One,* I had visited (again, for the first time, other than in relation to live exposure to a couple of tracks at a single concert), *The Yes Album* and *Fragile* (1971). The pre-world even to these creations, which had been developed on a much smaller scale and with different resources to their three large-scale successors, was evidently going to be another experience altogether. The first two albums had been buried by an avalanche of media appreciation for the third and fourth. Yet one of the many rewards of listening to Yes music is that no one album ever sounds quite as one might anticipate, let alone in terms of what has occurred previously or what will happen subsequently. Which was precisely my ahistorical point of entry to the LP/CD, *Yes.*

The tracks of our years

It seems appropriate that the band's first ever album track should indeed be entitled 'Beyond and Before', a piece penned by Chris Squire in collaboration with his former partner in psychedelic pioneers, Mabel Greer's Toyshop, Clive Bayley. It perfectly captures the panoramic hindsight and foresight that has characterised Yes music at its best, but which has deserted them somewhat in moments of turmoil and uncertainty. Indeed in the first minute and ten seconds of the song you have pretty much a prospectus for what the group was to aim at. A scything guitar opener, full of controlled dissonance; propulsive and thundering (yet tuneful) bass, scat vocal harmonies; a burst of melodic flare and an opening verse of rhapsodic anticipation: "Sparkling trees of silver foam cast shadows in winter home/Swaying branches breaking sound, lonely forest trembling ground." The bridge is positively Beatlesque ("It seems like the end of my life"), the verse-chorus is redelivered in percussion-punctuated acapella, before Banks drives towards an electric/acoustic conclusion suspended on a quieter, pastoral reprise (3:55–4:40). A great deal of imagination and development packed into just under five minutes.

By contrast, 'I See You', adapted from the original version by American band the Byrds (written by Jim McGuinn and David Crosby), is a much lighter, foot-tapping affair, propelled forward on a jaunty, jazzy theme with rich vocal harmony and bell-like guitar flourishes. At 1:14 and again at 1:30 and onwards, Jon Anderson's voice, high and smoky, asserts itself strongly for the first time on the album, imposing the narrative arc of the song. Banks comes in just after 2:30 full of angular buzz, and then a clean, clear tone that would later become a Yes hallmark with Steve Howe. From 3:00 the classical and jazz influences and inflections, with hints of polyphony, shape a guitar and percussion interlude, full of youthful enthusiasm. This is a listening as well as a playing band. There is a minute of heaviness and intensity before the final reprise of the main theme and crashing finale. Another unexpected journey has taken place. "[T]he 1968 equivalent of Aphex Twin remixing REM", suggested reviewer Joy Shapes at Discogs in 2010!

The third track, 'Yesterday and Today', showcases Anderson's distinctive voice accompanied principally by piano, vibraphone and acoustic guitar – an unusual choice of instrumentation. This is a quite different mood and sound shape to what has gone before. The tune is pleasant enough, but not especially memorable or distinct. But you can almost hear the nightclub shimmer around the vocals, from the choirboy who has had one too many cigarettes around the back of the stage or studio.

'Looking Around' was a staple of early Yes performances, and with its straight-ahead quality you can soon hear why. That said, its pitching is pleasingly odd for a proto-rock song. As Banks remarked to interviewer Tim Morse in 1994: "We could never figure out what key it was in". Atmospheric stabs of organ (3:18) represent a haunting climax, leading into a final vocal flourish and a three-point turn of an ending.

Bill Bruford, schooled in jazz, reckons that the title of 'Harold Land' must have come from the tenor saxophonist of the same name, but no one else seems quite to remember it that way. Certainly, neither the music nor the lyric bears any resemblance to Land's dark tone and experiments in modalism. For me, the highlight of the song is the concluding instrumental break at 5:09, which I could happily bear to hear further extemporised, as occasionally is reported to have happened live.

Next up is Yes's take on an early Beatles number, 'Every Little Thing'. Full of instrumental intensity, this arrangement moves far from the playfulness of the original. Indeed the main theme (and a sly little reference to 'Day Tripper') only emerges definitively at 1:48. "We played it live at a ridiculous speed", Banks recalled later. There's a certain artistic chemistry here which suggests not just what Yes are capable of bringing to inherited material, but also the rich blending of disparate musical elements and dynamic changes that will be a signature of their later style. Interestingly, the Anderson / Howe / Squire / Wakeman / White line-up reprised this song, 34 years after it was last performed, for the US leg of their 2004 tour.

As a first presentation of Yes to a new listenership, 'Sweetness' (an Anderson song, supplemented by Chris Squire and Clive Bailey, which is as every bit as cloying as its title suggests) hardly gave the listening public a decent clue as to what the band was going to be about. Not a bad song, and typically well crafted – but not a standout slice of pop, either. A typical record company choice, in other words. It subsequently featured in the comedy drama film *Buffalo '66* (released in 1998), the directorial debut of Vincent Gallo.

By contrast, Yes signed out their debut with an early environmental anthem, 'Survival', which combines instrumental flair and a strong melodic line, and was to resurface as a fragment in a medley made famous by the 1978 'In the Round' tour. Banks' penchant for guitar effects and Bruford's vibes are in evidence in the strong instrumental opening, before a fade into the acoustic-led ballad (1:25). The vocal line is poignantly saccharine, in contrast to the lyrical emphasis on the death-born impulse towards the natural struggle for life ("yesterdays endings will tomorrow life give you"). Clocking in at 6:19 this was the band's most extended workout so far, ending with the instrumentalists swapping a crisp five-note figure around to frame the suitably vague, if upbeat, conclusion that "we're all going somewhere". Indeed, but where exactly, on the strength of this showcase of eight quite different songs?

An emerging musical force

AMG Records' Bruce Eder was upbeat, looking back:

> "Yes' debut album is surprisingly strong, given the inexperience of all those involved at the time. In an era when psychedelic meanderings were the order of the day, Yes delivered a surprisingly focused and exciting record that covered lots of bases (perhaps too many) in presenting their sound."

Critic Lester Bangs, later a excoriating hater of progressive rock, reviewed the record favourably in *Rolling Stone*, writing in February 1970 that it was "the kind of album that sometimes insinuates itself into your routine with a totally unexpected thrust of musical power." However, Bill Bruford's verdict, with the benefit of hindsight in August 2010, was a little more sober:

> So, all in all, Yes' first was a simple, naïve affair. A beginners' album which got us some headway, and most importantly gave the budding Anderson–Squire writing partnership its first recorded results. It sold poorly after great reviews.

The original *Yes* album was remastered on CD by Atlantic Records on 1994, and then in 2003 by Rhino Records with six bonus tracks, four previously unreleased. There is an early version and a single reduction of Yes's fine take on Stephen Stills' 'Everydays' (which was to appear in full form on the next release), plus two prototype versions of 'Dear Father' (a 1969 EP promo and 1970 B-side for 'Sweet Dreams'), and then two versions (timed at 7:09 and 8:02 respectively) of the band's rearrangement of Leonard Bernstein's 'Something's Coming', from *West Side Story*. 'Dear Father' subsequently appeared on the February 1975 'early Yes' compilation, *Yesterdays*, which was in fact my own introduction to that era – and their amazing version of Paul Simon's 'America'. With plentiful use of orchestra and a strong Beatles influence, the song sounds too derivative for my ear, but it has enjoyed something of a revival of interest among aficionados of the band in recent years.

The absolute standout addition, however, is 'Something's Coming'. Writing in 1995–1996, Bill Martin (*Music of Yes: Structure and Vision in Progressive Rock*) suggested that it was 'not successful' and that it was a good thing in retrospect that the band did not write or cover more 'show tunes' of the Bernstein and Sondheim variety. In theory I can understand that. But Bill did not have the advantage at that stage of hearing this remaster. It is outstanding, capturing the live energy of Yes in a way that other recordings from this era do not. There's an extremely artful drum solo, pace and fluidity, energetic syncopation and vocal dexterity to this version of a classic popular music standard. The band bring all their instrumental and lyrical resources to this one, pushing as far as they can go until the next shape of the ensemble emerges chrysalis-like from the shell. 'Something's Coming' is well worth repeated listening to pick up the subtleties and musical quotations (several of them) contained within.

As a footnote on early Yes, *Something's Coming: The BBC Recordings 1969-1970* is a compilation of the only live recordings to feature the band's original line-up – Jon Anderson (vocals), Peter Banks (guitars), Tony Kaye (organ), Chris Squire (bass) and Bill Bruford (drums). It is a bringing together of Yes's early performances on BBC radio. The two-disc set features liner notes by Banks, who was moved on from the band shortly after these recordings were made. The album was released only in 1997, with supervision and notes by the guitarist. The US edition (Purple Pyramid, Cleopatra Records) is entitled *Beyond and Before: BBC Recordings 1969-1970*.

Chapter 3
Wake Up and Dream
(1970–1972)

> Music is everybody's business. It's only publishers who think some people own it.
>
> – John Lennon

Clearly, things could not stand still artistically for the embryonic Yes after a musically promising but commercially limited debut. And they did not. Recognising that their studio sound lacked the power they evidenced on stage, and the breadth and depth they aspired to compositionally, Yes decided to draft in an orchestra for the follow-up album, *Time and a Word*, recorded in about six weeks at the end of 1969 and the beginning of the following year, and released on 24 July 1970. Or at least Jon Anderson decided that, after discussion with bassist Chris Squire and new producer Tony Colton. Guitarist Peter Banks and organist–pianist Tony Kaye, who other band members felt was being resistant to the new synthesised keyboards currently working their way into the adventurous end of the music scene, were none-too-pleased at this orchestral manoeuvring in the dark. But Anderson, in particular, felt that they were not offering the kind of instrumental soundscape the band needed for the material he was throwing at them, and an experiment with a Mellotron (an electro-mechanical, polyphonic tape replay keyboard first developed in 1963) had not worked.

Opportunity knocks?

A string section and a brass section comprising students from the Royal College of Music were therefore duly hired to perform arrangements written and conducted by Tony Cox, and engineered by Gerald Chevin. That choice is announced right at the beginning of the album as lush, loud, swirling strings introduce an ambitious cover version of Ritchie Havens' powerful 'No Opportunity Necessary, No Experience Needed', using a theme taken from the soundtrack to the 1958 Western movie, *The Big Country*, by Jerome Moross. The result is frankly bizarre ... or intriguing, depending on your perspective. Mine is still more towards the former. That said, 'No Opportunity' featured a monstrously enveloping bass line from Squire, a driving melodic theme prefigured by opening organ chords that stab the senses, angular guitar breaks, Anderson declaiming in a lower register than his characteristic alto-tenor, that cowboy theme reappearing, and rockier drumming than Bruford has previously been known for on record. It was in many respects a preposterous combination, but, unexpectedly, it worked. Unsurprisingly, Yes often used the song as an opener. "If we can get that right, we can get anything right," Banks once claimed.

Having begun with a big, bold track whose scale belied its 4' 48" length, the band continued with another forceful statement. 'Then' uses a wide range of dynamic treatments (less than common for rock groups in those days) and a lingeringly questioning lyrical approach ("souls will be complicated, life will be consummated ... then." It emerges from sonic distance before establishing a groove. The orchestra blends well with the top end of the organ and guitar on this occasion, lending a genuine breadth to the music. This is one of the tracks on which the strings seem to me to work, not standing out like a plucked bow as they do on 'No Opportunity'. The bass and drum ostinato (2:30 onwards) has shades of Crimson in it, incidentally. There's a deliciously brief Hammond lick (2:52 then 3:10) before band and instrumentalists reprise the main riff into more organ, insistent bass and drums, a blast from the brass, and a held organ chord seguing into a dreamy interlude. The mood quietens. Banks uses delayed guitar (4:30). Anderson's achingly beautiful vocal entry captures the mood hauntingly. "Love is the only answer, hate is the root of cancer ... then." Bruford uses splashes of percussion to add to the atmosphere, and then thunders into the wonderfully discordant and disturbing climax. A 5-minute 44-second poem in sound.

The poetic sensibility continues into a fabulous, extended and jazzy (6' 12") reworking of Stephen Stills' song 'Everydays', fusing languid, dream-like sequences with a vigorous instrumental interlude. The string arrangement is well designed, though perhaps a little overstated. The drum brushes are pleasingly evocative. Jon Anderson's singing has a lingering, angelic, yet knowing and raspy quality, the sophistication of which belies his years. It is simultaneously melancholic and summery, underpinned by echoing organ and strings. Banks adds guitar effects, and then we are projected from a lazy, hazy day into (2:20) a propelling, aggressive instrumental in which bass, drums, guitar and organ unleash a wildly expansive orgy of delight in 3/4 or 6/8. Strings and organ double up, and there's a mini-quote from 'Greensleeves', before (4:40) the deceptive pastoral calm, underwritten by just a hint of menace, is restored. "Well, well, well ... another day," and we are returned to the early atmosphere and a startled, bass-conveyed ending.

Next up is the relatively straightforward and anthemic 'Sweet Dreams', re-establishing the more popular end of the band's credentials. Future Yes guitarist Trevor Rabin particularly liked this song, getting the band to perform it in concert many years later during the *90125* tour (1984). It was also performed during the mid-seventies, when Yes was otherwise in its most complex musical phase, once more by Anderson/Bruford/Wakeman/Howe (ABWH) in 1989 and 1990, and then again by reformed classic Yes in 2004.

Alongside 'Everydays', the other standout track for me on *Time and a Word* is 'The Prophet' (6' 34"), which marks another significant step forward from the first album, and begins to connect with the giant leap that will come with *The Yes Album*. Warning against the lure of the flawed, charismatic leader, the extended song borrows a theme from 'Jupiter, the Bringer of Jollity' from composer Gustav Holst's *The Planets* suite. It shows Jon Anderson incorporating snatches of themes and ideas from classical music, to which he was listening regularly. As the singer and lyricist explained to *Record Review* in 1982:

> I had speakers at the bottom of my bed, blasting out classical music all the time. So in one ear there was rock, and in the other ear was the classics. I was interested in opening up the sound of the band.

This piece illustrates the impact of that approach very well. It is multi-layered and involves a number of tempo and key changes early on. It is very powerful and purposeful. Bill Bruford nonetheless warned himself, in a *Melody Maker* interview in 1970, that "I suppose it's very easy to be too clever". Playing less became his watchword when he eventually made the switch from Yes to King Crimson.

'Clear Days' was perhaps intended to be Anderson's 'Eleanor Rigby' moment, as Banks (less than flatteringly) suggested to interviewer Tim Morse in 1994. The lyrical and string styles do not altogether hit it off, and this can perhaps be considered the least successful musical outcome on the album. But it was a brave move, with a surprising (and to my ears, pleasing) degree of chromaticism in the string parts, especially towards the end. Elvis Costello and the Brodsky String Quartet were to have more success with this kind of combination – though to far from universal acclaim – in *The Juliet Letters* in 1993.

The last two tracks on the album, which had followed its predecessor's pattern of six original compositions and two covers, subsequently became Yes staples – the contrasting 'Astral Traveller' and the eponymous 'Time and a Word'. The former captures the post-psychedelic to progressive atmosphere effectively. Just under six minutes long, Tony Kaye utilises a strong Leslie speaker effect for his M-100 organ, while Anderson trails a propulsive bass and drum theme and Banks has one of his finest guitar outings with the band. The fast, contrapuntal, classically styled instrumental interlude from 2:09 to 2:52 is one of my favourite 'formative Yes' moments. Then the guitarist takes over, glazing the development so far with a sinewy and brash solo, underpinned by organ and the gutsy rhythm section. The continuously ascending transition (3:55) back to the main riff (4:18) is masterfully conveyed. Bruford has subsequently gently chastised himself for overplaying a stack of drum tropes on this song, but it is surely relatively easy for the rest of us to forgive the youthful exuberance on such a joyous track. Not that Peter Banks ever forgave the producer for allowing David Foster's primitive acoustic guitar to remain on 'Time and a Word' when the guide tracks were only partially removed. The song has a strong melody, and has survived Yes setlists right through to 2015–17 because of its powerfully nostalgic feel. Not one of my personal favourites, but I can nevertheless see the appeal. It captures a mood and a moment in the balladry of formative Yes.

A changing musical landscape
After *Time and a Word*, it was all change again. Well, not 'all', perhaps, but certainly the first in a series of transitions in personnel that was to become something of a revolving door over time, driven both by musical and extra-musical considerations. The circumstances behind Peter Banks' departure from Yes will

probably never be finally agreed, but sadly it left the now late guitarist with a good deal of dissatisfaction and bitterness over the coming years. In his place came the equally self-taught but highly accomplished Steve Howe, whose distinctive tone, style and growing portfolio was shaped outwith the mainstream blues-rock guitar approach. Instead, it was country finger-picking (Chet Atkins), virtuosic jazz (Wes Montgomery, Jim Hall) and Baroque music (Dowland, Vivaldi, plus the playing of Segovia) that fed his psychedelic pop and rock imagination with all kinds of different ideas ... a number of which were about to find a home on two ground-breaking releases, *The Yes Album* and the iconic *Fragile*.

The Yes Album was recorded between the summer and autumn of 1970, and released in February 1971. Given the relative lack of sales of the first two LPs, it could easily not have been, as Bill Martin observes in his liner notes for the 2003 expanded and remastered CD release. Yes could have been strangled almost at birth. But, as John Lennon observed, music rightly belongs to people before business, and thankfully music won out in this instance. The arrival of Howe, the presence of Eddy Offord as producer (he had been involved with *Time and a Word*, but began to exercise real influence now) and the inspiration derived from rehearsals at Langley Farm in the English west country (subsequently bought by the Howe family) meant that a fresh synergy had taken hold by the time the band was ready to record at Advision Studios once again.

The Yes Album opens with Yes's most powerful and distinctive musical statement yet. 'Yours Is No Disgrace' launched itself into the world on the back of another staccato Western theme, making it something of a 'No Opportunity' mark two in that regard, if few others. The lyric was written by Jon Anderson with the late David Foster, taking as its subject the plight of young soldiers caught up in the Vietnam War. Not a fully-fledged anti-war song, 'Yours Is No Disgrace' is nevertheless sanguine about the horrors of war, while ever hopeful about the capacity of the human spirit to rise above the blood and anguish. Anderson paints feelings with words ("death defying, mutilated, armies gather near") and technology with animalistic imagery ("shining, flying, purple wolfhound"). Musically, the piece projects itself on the foundations of fierce, propelling bass and drums, overlaid with a delicate guitar figure on which Howe's trademark Gibson ES-175 semi-acoustic rings out. Kaye's new, rasping B-3 organ brings the flow to an abrupt end (1:24) as a prelude to Anderson's poignant vocals. Chris Squire's walking bass part (3:16) is especially evocative. Here, then, are the first in a series of twists, turns and climaxes throughout a compelling sonic melodrama lasting a little under ten minutes – and expanded by several more minutes in live performance, as the guitar and bass solos, elaborating and developing existing melodic themes, are expanded. For me the best recorded rendition of the song is to be found on the *House of Yes* live CD (1999), where the power, delicacy, dynamics and musical elaboration so characteristic of Yes across the years is beautifully and powerfully held in balance.

Next up is Steve Howe's signature guitar piece, 'Clap', written the night before the birth of his son Dylan (now an established and accomplished jazz drummer who has also played live with Yes). On *The Yes Album* the version included was recorded live at the Lyceum Theatre in London on 17 July 1970. A studio version was featured as a bonus track on the 2003 remaster and 2014 'definitive edition', along with a rather unnecessary single edit again in 2014. The acoustic piece, performed on Howe's Martin 00-18 (the other guitar he used on this album, and throughout his career) is a homage to Chet Atkins and reminiscent also of Mason Williams' famous tune, 'Classical Gas'. It illustrates the then new Yes man's artistry and dexterity, as well as bringing a fresh and unexpected country flavour into the band.

The third song on the album, again clocking in at 9' 29" (and up to 14 minutes live, with the often bombastic expansion of the third section), is 'Starship Trooper', another tune seen across the years as a Yes classic. There is a distinctive chord progression at the heart of the piece – one that Tony Kaye once proclaimed himself "sick of", but which an organ scholar friend of mine says first made him sit up and pay real attention to the band as a student. Anderson took the title from a 1959 science fiction novel by Robert Heinlein, though the song otherwise has nothing to do with the book. Instead, it is somewhat about the guardianship of Mother Earth and the quest for the divine inside and out, according to the lyricist. The opening section, 'Life Seeker', sets out the main musical themes, segueing into another jazzy sequence (1:53) before a recapitulation and restatement (2:37). Howe's snappy acoustic guitar introduces a breezy but questioning interlude ('Disillusion') ahead of a suspended, harmonised, instrumental climax (4:17). There is a brief restatement of the main theme, and then a sudden twist into the finale, 'Würm', which Howe brought from a previous composition. Introduced with a few quiet, simple notes on guitar, it climbs and builds into something monumentally dramatic, carried in live performance by a series of instrumental solos. In fact the chord progression starts halfway through the section, and it takes 54 measures before the soloing starts. On the recording, 'Starship Trooper' ends by fading to silence, leaving you wanting more. The 'less is more' approach has often been lost in concert, it has to be said, as the piece is utilised – understandably – as a thundering, crowd-shattering encore. As an aside, it has been noted that the 'Würm' theme has been quoted by Nirvana on 'Heart Shaped Box', among others.

How do you follow that? In this case with another popular classic, 'I've Seen All Good People' (6' 56"), which effects an unlikely fusion of what is essentially a tastefully rendered acoustic ballad ('Your Move') with a repeated and extended blues-inflected riff ('All Good People') by means of a rousing, vocally accompanied organ crescendo (2:49–3:20) more suited to a church or concert hall than the bridge in this unlikely musical compendium. For the longstanding Yes listener the familiarity of this piece (once again, routinely extended for instrumental impact in concert) may detract from an awareness of how new and different it was when it first appeared. The sweet harmony vocals on the opening section apparently led Atlantic Records, viewing their protégés from across the ocean, to consider Yes to be "a kind of English folk act" at one point. As for the foot-stomping 'All Good People', it has a blues feel (unusually for Yes) but makes its impact by inserting a major third rather than a minor third, with a C# before the A in the riff. It is through such simple means that the band, in this case Chris Squire, is able to produce something at once familiar and different – the root, I believe, to its lure and appeal.

Perhaps the forgotten song on The Yes Album is the tiny (3' 15") but well formed miniature, 'A Venture', which opens with distant, echoing piano and a delicate guitar figure. Then drums and bass (a pentatonic few notes) kick in to introduce a gently swinging tune, the briefest of choruses ("Couldn't hide away … hide away") and a shift of key and melody towards a brighter tone – before returning to the dominant theme with a staccato twist. The instrumental resolution revolves around a receding piano and bass extemporisation rejoined by the guitar. 'A Venture' is an underrated gem. There is also a delightfully extended version (4' 48") that ends quite unexpectedly with a display of bluesy dissonance. Yes are looking to use every effect to make their impact at this crucially developmental phase in their musical lifecycle.

The final entry on the band's third album is another (by now) established standard, 'Perpetual Change', a title that seems entirely emblematic of Yes's ever-changing musical journey. With its urgent, insistent, declamatory 5-5-3-5 opening pattern, this gorgeous piece ('song' seems too limiting by this stage) is all about dramatic effect, contrast, tension and release. While the instrumental work has power and poise, the lyrical content is light, airy and pastoral in its delivery: "I see the coldness in the night / and watch the hills roll out of sight". But 'Perpetual Change' has every intention of living up to the promise of its title. As Bill Bruford recalls (Morse, 1994):

> We were always looking for a couple of lines to go against each other, a bit of counterpoint.

The employing of contrapuntal technique was definitely an art school twist. So was the use of 7/4 for the chorus and a double-time version to follow and accompany it, synching together in a curious battle of assertion and counter-assertion. A very different era of Yes, the *Talk* line-up featuring Trevor Rabin, was to use part of this song as an opener on their 1994 American and South American tours, after two brief experiments ten years before (Pennsylvania and Ohio, 1984). The Anderson/Rabin/Wakeman iteration of the band also picked it up in 2016 and 2017.

The great leap forward

The Yes Album undoubtedly represented significant progress for Yes. Lauded even by those who subsequently became disenchanted with progressive rock, it set new standards of composition, arrangement and instrumentation in the rock field. This band sounded like no other and was now on a sharp ascension to even headier climbs, marked in the first instance by their fourth album, *Fragile*, which many regard as a core statement of what they are about musically. Recorded around September 1971, released in November that year and toured into 1972, the *Fragile* album was the first to feature new keyboard star Rick Wakeman, who brought the kind of flamboyance, technological advancement and instrumental colour (electric piano, harpsichord, Mellotron and MiniMoog synthesisers) which the departing Tony Kaye appeared unable to contend with at this stage. Wakeman was also a mean Hammond organ player and brought compositional and arranging skills (as well as the ability to score) picked up from his short but formative time at the Royal College of Music in London. Another forward leap was on the cards.

The opener on *Fragile* is the song that over the years has become virtually the Yes national anthem, 'Roundabout'. Penned by Anderson and Howe, with important instrumental contributions from the rest of the band, 'Roundabout', lasting 8' 30" on disc, is practically a one-stop mission statement for Yes. The unusual opening was created by recording a piano note and playing it backwards. More complicated than it sounds at the time. Steve Howe, who conceived his parts as a kind of wordless guitar suite, then hints at the major themes on his Martin acoustic, before the bass and drums launch into the main, swaggering tune. The highly distinctive bass sound was achieved by Chris Squire ghosting his trebly Rickenbacker with a miked-up Gibson electric guitar to achieve an effect that was simultaneously metallic yet rounded. The sometimes derided lyrics to the song derive from a journey back to Glasgow from Aviemore, in which both the mist-coated scenery ("mountains climb out of the sky") and the twisting road with its byways and roundabouts created an extended metaphor for the song. Rick Wakeman's organ solo, which swings without any noticeable reference to jazz, is another highlight, along with the scat acapella ending (a combination of notes repeated eight times, with variation). It is a tour-de-force that combines popular appeal with clever instrumental effects and a structure that hints at classical form without aping it. It was to become Yes's first 'hit', with radio reductions produced to encourage airplay. The foundations of the song were reportedly laid during Rick Wakeman's first day at Advision Studios. Peter Banks, who left after *Time and a Word* subsequently claimed to have forged the main riff around Em, F#m and G. Others may dispute that.

Next up on *Fragile* are the first two of five brief vignettes, "individual ideas, personally arranged and organised" by the five band members. Solo statements from the musicians, if you like, augmented by the others as requested. It makes sense to tackle them as a group of pieces. Jon Anderson's 'We Have Heaven' features a range of vocal overlays harmonising two simple melodies. It utilises a sixteen-track tape machine, and sound effects ranging from bombs, to echoes, to receding footsteps. In some ways this track establishes the ground that Anderson would use for his first (and, for many, defining) self-created solo album, *Olias of Sunhillow* (1976). By contrast, Rick Wakeman had little choice as to what he could do. Restricted by publishing rights from using a piece called 'Handle with Care' that eventually emerged as 'Catherine of Aragon' on his best-selling solo instrumental album, *The Six Wives of Henry VIII* (1973), the keyboard player returned to classical roots for a synthesised version of excerpts from the third movement of Brahms' Fourth Symphony (Op 96). His own verdict on 'Cans and Brahms' was that it was "dreadful". Viewed retrospectively it has a certain period curiosity. Its originator performed it live across five nights in Australia (Sydney and Melbourne) in 1973. Then Geoff Downes revived it as part of a full rendering of the *Fragile* album throughout a series of US and European dates in 2014 and 2016.

The irascible Bill Bruford took an entirely different tack with his contribution. His 'Five Per Cent for Nothing' (a dig at their manager, for which he subsequently apologised) lasts just 35 seconds, but packs in all the expected rhythmic complexity. It was his first stab at solo composition, and was, he said in 1995, "completely naïve". I still find it enjoyable and suitably tongue-in-cheek, though Alan White, who succeeded Bruford on the drum riser, may have had a different opinion after tackling its decidedly angular charm live in 2014 and 2016!

The final two vignettes were perhaps the strongest on the album. Chris Squire's 'The Fish (Schindleria Praematurus)' stayed with him throughout the whole of his career, adapted in a number of ways in live solo slots. It is almost a singular, compressed summary of his bass talents – haunting, unpredictable, showy and exploiting moods and potentials in his instrument that bypassed its pedestrian role in most areas of rock music to that point. The title combines Squire's nickname (coined for long stints in the bath, apparently) and the name of what is supposed to be one of the smallest prehistoric fish in the world ... ironic, given the large bassman's epic pretensions, for which he was both mocked and admired. The piece itself emerges out of Steve Howe's guitar harmonics from the preceding song, "Long Distance Runaround." Indeed, it could almost be seen as an extension of that tune. Bill Bruford provides a steady syncopation of hi-hat and snare to accompany short bass stabs that give way to Squire's main riff, punctuated, overlaid and elaborated as it proceeds. Cowbell and mbira add to the colour. An echoey, floating effect is created on bass, amplified by Howe's wah-wah pedal effect. Then a tambourine enters. Squire's bass is both delayed and doubled. The tune builds towards the climactic entry of the eight-syllable mantra, "Schindleria Praematurus," which the bass player had searched for as a departure point for his piece. It's a wonderful, highly atmospheric piece of sound modelling.

Last but not least, before we return to the remaining three group compositions, is Steve Howe's lovely classical/flamenco piece, 'Mood for a Day', structured on a simple B minor motif played in 3/4 on a Conde guitar. A curious blend of Baroque, lullaby, flamenco and folk strum, it carries a beautiful tune through a pleasing set of ornamentations. Unlike classical players, Howe mostly uses his thumb and index finger to pick out highlighted parts, utilising his self-generated technique to good effect. There is delicacy, feeling and atmosphere in this little piece, which never tires to my ear. It also offers a bright, refreshing interlude on an otherwise busy album.

'Long Distance Runaround' (3' 30"), the next group outing, is a jaunty little song about human (and apparently, in Jon Anderson's mind, religious) promise and betrayal. Considered apiece with instrumental 'The Fish', it clocks in at 6' 09". Instrumentally, its distinctive feature is Wakeman's RMI 368 Electric Piano, grand piano and harpsichord. It is worth noting that the tune shifts keys between A minor and B minor and is polymetric in the verses. The drums are in 5/8, while the rest of the group is in 4/4. Little tricks like this are what have enabled Yes, over the years, to alternate passing off the complex as straightforward, and the straightforward as complex – retaining a balance and synergy between 'head music' and 'foot music'. In February 2011 it was pointed out on Bill Bruford's online forum that the first measure of 'Long Distance Runaround' bears something of a resemblance to a line in jazz saxophonist and composer Charlie Parker's 'Ornithology'. The drummer responded:

> To my certain knowledge the Parker tune was never mentioned in rehearsal, and I doubt Rick Wakeman would have known it, but Steve Howe might have ingested it though his blood stream.

Like Bruford, Howe was a modern jazz listener. Wakeman was most definitely not.

Next up on this landmark album is the striking 'South Side of the Sky', which combines a howling wind, a rocky texture and a dark and brooding theme (death by exposure, the rawness of nature) with a contrastingly delicate piano interlude – plus a beautiful, wordless vocal harmony section from 3:19 to 5:42. The overall mood is ambiguous, both musically and lyrically ("The moments seemed lost in all the noise / A snow storm, a stimulating voice / Of warmth of the sky, of warmth when you die.") Yet the realisation of it is disarmingly simple, with Chris Squire, for example, riffing on a single open string at one point. As is always the case in the best Yes music, the means are there to achieve clear ends. It is not the case, as some of their critics have been rather too quick to aver over the years, that they pursued virtuosity or complexity for their own sake. Such elements are there, when they are, for a reason. Likewise the directness. The coherence of the songs on this album is testimony to that.

Fragile was, of course, also the record that introduced 'Heart of the Sunrise', a perennial of Yes concert favourite, to the world. This was another early Rick Wakeman contribution to the band, introducing the group to recapitulation, an element of the sonata form he had absorbed at music school before dashing off to do sessions with the likes of David Bowie ('Life on Mars') and Cat Stevens ('Morning Has Broken'). The band had also been spurred on to greater musical achievement by listening to King Crimson, as we noted in the last Chapter. And that certainly included the shuddering, fast, impulsive ostinato section on '21st Century Schizoid Man', from *In The Court of the Crimson King* (1970). You can hear clear echoes of it in the frantic opening instrumental section of 'Heart of the Sunrise', which is repeated three times (punctuated after the first iteration by Chris Squire's lingering bass solo), and reprised later, towards the climax of the song. It alternates between 6/8 and 3/4. Bill Bruford's drumming is crisp, angular and cleverly decorated throughout. The song itself ushers in a significant change in mood, dynamics and tempo at 3:24. A paean to both nature (the energy of the sunrise) and the relational power of love, it also references a sense of disorientation brought on by urban life ("I feel lost in the city..."). The guitar and organ-led interlude in 5/8 (4:44) punctuates the lyrical build up, which continues at 5:01, gathering intensity and modulating a couple of times into the recapitulation. Howe's guitar intervention (7:52) creates a suitable bridge to Wakeman's piano motif (8:07) in 9/8. We then return to the main texture of the song, punctuated by other little reprises (9:19), before a final, climactic rendering of the lyrical theme and a concluding flourish from the opening riff.

At 10′ 35″, 'Heart of the Sunrise' was the longest Yes song to date, the culmination of another pace-setting album, and an example of the way the band could so effectively elide simplicity and sophistication in a lengthy, elliptical and enticing musical statement. Well crafted and arranged, it uses some conventions and tricks from western art music, while clearly being in the rock mode. In addition to his ability to shape and develop the music in ways that allowed Yes to expand, Rick Wakeman also brought instrumental colour to the whole. The Moog, for bright bursts, but especially the Mellotron (6:31) for orchestral texture. Indeed, this is probably the track that started to gain Yes a reputation in some quarters as pioneers of 'symphonic rock' (a not altogether helpful term, in my estimation – see Chapter 14).

All in all then, *The Yes Album* and *Fragile* were huge steps into the future for Yes. The composition and instrumentation was strong on both. The arrangements were getting better by the hour. Eddy Offord, virtually a sixth member of the band by this point, was definitely in his stride production-wise. The studio equipment and multi-tracking facilities were improving all the time. 'Heart of the Sunrise', especially, represented a new level of variation and subtlety, alongside power and conviction, in Yes music. The scene was well and truly set for the masterpiece that was to come in 1972.

Chapter 4
Seasons Will Pass You By
(*Close to the Edge*)

A seasoned witch could call you from the depths of your disgrace
And rearrange your liver to the solid mental grace
And achieve it all with music that came quickly from afar
And taste the fruit of man recorded losing all against the hour

– the opening stanza of 'Close to the Edge'

It was during a conversation over an evening meal about thirty-five years ago when I first heard the accusation, not infrequently repeated since, that "Yes is a rock band for people who don't really like rock music." At the time I quite enjoyed that claim; revelled in it, even. Now I have rather more mixed reactions. On the one hand, a quick listen to the music (especially live) and a look at the demographics of Yes audiences would soon disprove it. Indeed, subsequent tours with the likes of Kansas, Asia and Styx might put the band rather too solidly into the 'rock mainstream' for many of its loftier advocates or critics. Similarly, when Yes went on the road in the US with Steven Wilson's highly-regarded band Porcupine Tree in 2002, many PT camp followers were unhappy to be associated with what they took as purveyors of backward-looking musical populism. So the association was duly excised from the undeniably hip PT website. However, Wilson is certainly an advocate of earlier Yes (especially the contrasting delights of *Close to the Edge, Tales From Topographic Oceans* and *Drama*) and has gone on to create acclaimed, groundbreaking 5.1 remixes for the band. All of which proves that judgements of the kind offered by my dinner companion depend heavily upon where you are situated when you make them, what your listening parameters are, and how much of a role fashion or its inversions might play in your estimation of music.

It is certainly true that Yes music, never less than eclectic in its influences and aspirations, has stretched and questioned many of the supposed norms of the idiom in which it is most clearly rooted. Moreover, defying "rock and roll orthodoxy" should hardly be an insult in an era where the narrowing commercial dictates of the music industry have all-too-often suffocated the creativity, dissent and diversion that are essential to any true artistic endeavour, especially if it dares to be labelled 'progressive'. That is, the desire to expand the vocabulary and grammar of music, rather than simply to fill the coffers of recording company executives. In this sense, we might take the "anti-rock" accusations, superficial though many of them are, to be something of a merited compliment to Yes. In spite of their frailties and vulnerabilities, the band surely helped to break a limiting rock mould in their defining epoch, even if some of the sludge coming out of that mould subsequently attached itself to their coat tails.

The creation of *Close to the Edge*
Will Romano (2017) has devoted a whole book to understanding the significance of the arrival of *Close to the Edge*. A good read it is, too. I will have to be briefer, before turning to a reconsideration of the actual recorded notes. In its own time, the three three-track *Close to the Edge* album (comprising the 18-minute-

plus title track, the mini-suite 'And You and I' and a hypnotic 'Siberian Khatru') represented far more than another step forwards for Yes. It was a quantum shift for the band, and indeed for the whole fast-expanding genre of progressive rock which it was soon deemed not just to be part, but an archetype for. That it did so is at least as much the outcome of happenstance as any master strategy, if the stories about how it was recorded are anything to go by. In its earlier years, Yes was a 'working band', constantly passing through the revolving doors of clubs, halls and university venues up and down the nation, and occasionally meandering around Germany and other European countries. The question of how this musical unit could find enough time and chemistry to bring a worthwhile new album to existence after the peak achieved in 1971/2 by *Fragile* and its advertising standard-bearer, 'Roundabout', was a moot one.

Bill Bruford observes:

The process in the older rock groups has been likened to four architects designing the same building, or four novelists trying to collaborate on one book. There was inevitably a lot of horse-trading – 'I've got this great chorus and riff, but you hate my riff. I could live with your words, which I don't care for, if you could think again about my riff'. Try doing that with four creatively muscular people in one room, and life can get tough.

And tough it was, by all accounts. Notes were indeed argued over. Musical ideas were traded and bargained. Blows were nearly struck (or actually were, according to some). The drummer wanted to get on with it. The bass player wanted to fine-tune his couple of bars, again and again. And all the while, Anderson was firing them forward, Offord was gluing and re-gluing bits of tape, and Howe and Wakeman were bringing ideas aplenty into the mix as Yes recorded, broke the equipment down, played some gigs, set up again, tried to pick up the thread and then repeated the process. It was amazing that the thing got finished, let alone that it turned out to be a masterpiece. Accounts within the band differ, of course. We will never know what kind of alchemy was at work.

Close to the Edge was conceived and pieced together between February and July 1972, with the band rehearsing together at the Una Billings School of Dance midway through the period and finally locating themselves in Advision Studios in June of that year. The finished product was eventually released in September. Eddy Offord was brought in as studio engineer and co-producer with the five members of the band. He helped create a unique architecture to the studio, with a performance platform intended to encourage the feel and energy of the live band, and a wooden booth for guitarist Steve Howe to enhance his sound. The resulting album has been described by music journalist Chris Welch, who witnessed the often-fractious recording sessions, as "a vast jigsaw of sound". The work began while Yes were finishing off their 'Fragile' tour (which ended in March 1972) and included recording rehearsals so as to try not to lose important ideas. Each section of the title track, in particular, was argued over and pieced together painstakingly, with apparently no clear idea about the final outcome. The somewhat anarchic process reflected both the relative inexperience and surging creative impulses of Anderson, Bruford, Howe, Squire, Wakeman and Offord at the time. It also renders even more extraordinary the dynamism and coherence of the final recording.

By the time they pieced together the 18' 50" 'Close to Edge', Yes had already generated compositions up to ten minutes long, but they had never attempted or achieved anything on this scale. For classical composers something in the region of 20 minutes might be thought of as a moderately sized suite, but in a rock world still dominated by three-minute verse and chorus style songs what Yes were tackling was hugely ambitious, a venture into unknown territory where the musical ideas would lead and the musicians would follow, essentially attempting to keep up with the fruits of their own imagination. The whole was assembled it seems, in ten or twelve roughly sixteen bar sections, which you can begin to identify if you analyse it closely. It turned out to be far from a forlorn exercise, and listening to the album today, some 46 years on, you can still feel the cumulative tension and release as the music surges forward and takes form.

Solid mental grace
The track 'Close to the Edge' takes its inspiration, theme and highly metaphoric lyrics from *Siddhartha* (1922), by German novelist Hermann Hesse. According to Jon Anderson, it also partly emerged from a dream about "passing on from this world to another" through the veil of death. Bill Bruford has commented that the title also reflects his sense of the state of the band at that time, poised on a creative precipice and with fracture always a real possibility. It was, indeed, the drummer's final album for the group until his brief and not altogether willing return to the band in 1991–2. The paradoxical phrase "solid mental grace" captures for me something of the essence of this album, this piece, and also of Yes as a creative musical consideration approaching the height of its powers. "All that is solid melts into air," Marx famously wrote in his *Communist Manifesto*. Fixed, fast-frozen relations from the past are re-forged in the foment of change. So it is with Yes's music at this time. There is a solidity to it, grounded (against some of its critics) in the visceral force of rock. But there is also a strong pull towards mental energy and the world of ideas, art and the mind. The two are held together by a certain grace and elegance that enables the music to transcend and transform its roots while remaining true to them.

It is the sound of nature and the forces of chaos out of which the music of 'Close to the Edge' emerges. *Musique concrète*, originating in the work of French composer Pierre Schaeffer and his associates at the Studio d'Essai in 1948, had already drawn the attention of the Beatles on *Sergeant Pepper* through the mediation of Karlheinz Stockhausen and others. So it was daring, but not original, for Yes (apparently inspired in this case by Wendy Carlos's *Sonic Seasonings*) to use a tape-loop involving cascading water, birdsong and a keyboard drone for the opening 'notes', building rapidly into a huge forest of sound until the band finally breaks in and responds (0:56) by unleashing a ferocious burst of instrumental intensity. The section through to 2:51, entitled 'The Solid Time of Change', originated in a group jam, and is punctuated twice by brief vocal expulsions that begin to establish a tonal centre in the midst of fast ascending notes exchanged between guitar and bass – part of what gives it a sense of controlled, directed chaos. The influence of the Mahavishnu Orchestra can most surely be detected.

Inter alia, Steve Howe's entry at 1:14 is accompanied by keyboard player Rick Wakeman playing the same riff as bassist Chris Squire in double-time, coming out of the D harmonic minor scale. Howe joins the theme at 2:00. From 2:58 to 3:51 the guitar takes the lead in articulating a major melodic theme for the next section and subsequent recapitulation, with important embellishments and refinements on bass, keyboards and drums. It has both a somewhat ecstatic aura and a thoughtful, lingering feel to it. Wakeman's organ introduces a moment of pause before the band syncopates into the opening two verses (4:00–4:35). The chorus ("close to the edge, down by a river") leads into the instrumental statement of a second theme (4:55–5:09), with Howe's crisp semi-acoustic guitar again taking the lead. There is a precision and cleanness of sound here that sets Yes well apart from the rock mainstream of the time, and the buzzing guitar effects preferred by Peter Banks in the earlier albums.

The new verse at 5:10 contains what for me are among the most evocative images Jon Anderson (whose later decline into cliché is notable by comparison) has ever produced. They revel in the joyous confusion of a blending of senses, seasons and temporal experience: "Crossed a line around the changes of the summer / Reaching out to call the colour of the sky / Passed around a moment clothed in mornings faster than we see." Howe's guitar weaves delicate patterns around these lyrical effusions, while Bruford's drums add texture and impulse. It's this kind of heady fusion that either draws you into Yes's sonic brew, or pushes you away from it. The re-entry of the chorus brings the opening section of the song (really a vocal/instrumental suite) to a close. At 6:05 Squire's urgent and irregular-rhythm bass thrusts introduce the second full section of the piece, 'Total Mass Retain'. The rhythmic play in the oncoming verse and chorus is clever but organic, and the synthesised keyboard colour provides contrast and light. At 7:10 there is another twist. "Sudden call shouldn't take away the startled memory," sings Anderson. "All in all the journey takes you all the way / as apart from any reality that you've ever seen and known." The intention to transport the listener, musically and lyrically, couldn't be clearer. Resistance is futile ... or perhaps fertile. A beautifully crafted bass figure (8:00–8:31) brings the declamation to an end, with Wakeman's keyboards lending contrapuntal weight and Bruford's percussion guiding it home into a swirl of atonal sound.

The 'I Get Up, I Get Down' section of 'Close to the Edge' emerges out of a richly textured wash of guitar and keyboard harmonics that seem to suspend time and carry us far away from the preceding urgency. In concert in the '70s this was often accompanied by dry ice to emphasise the transition visually and dramatically. Love it or loathe it, progressive rock at this level is performance art as well as musical construction. Again, we are in a floating tonal space, before Wakeman's higher-pitched organ stabs (9:50) recall attention and introduce the verse. Anderson's voice (10:08) soars above the palette of sounds. The intertwining and fused vocal and instrumental harmonies are richly emotional, with touches of dissonance. "In charge of who is there in charge of me? / Do I look on blindly and say I see?"

asks the singer. The answer comes dramatically at 12:00 with a surging climax and a rush of pipe organ, recorded at St Giles-without-Cripplegate Church in London's Barbican. If you are really trying, you can detect the tape edit. But the power of the moment is as overwhelming as it is intended to be. This is the first major climax of the song, taken to ever-greater heights by the organ (12:13–12:49) through the use of a gently swinging rhythm against forceful block chords. Anderson repeats the refrain, 'I get up, I get down', raising his voice at the end (13:05) to re-invite the organ back, drawing the whole to a crescendo that is brought to a shuddering conclusion in the most unexpected way – as Wakeman's Moog synthesiser crashes through to announce a dramatic new twist. At 13:56 "Moog notes flood the sonic foreground … blossom out of the church organ foundation, climb to the sky and cascade", writes Romano (2106). Three quick beats herald a rapid escalation of pace. Swathes of scraping synth galvanise a furious instrumental charge until Wakeman's Hammond signals yet another change of direction. It is one of the finest solos he has ever produced (15:01–15:50), combining perfectly with drums and bass to produce a jazzy feel that has nothing to do with jazz.

And so we arrive back at the 'Total Mass Retain' theme, seemingly having been dragged through a musical hedge backwards, yet actually propelled forward through a series of transitions that are at once stark and firmly glued together. It is difficult to explain what has happened, but it works. "The time between the notes relates the colour to the scene," sings Anderson. Maybe that, whatever it is, is what has happened! The lyrical images and metaphors simply pile up on one another at this point. We do not so much make sense of them; they try to make us into their own sense, clambering for, and beyond, meaning in the fourth section, 'Seasons of Man'. We are approaching the real climax here (16:34). "On the hill we viewed the silence of the valley / Called to witness cycles only of the past / And we reach all this with movements in between the said remark." We are as close to the edge of experience, understanding, life and death as we are ever going to get. The chorus re-enters in its fullest form, fusing the themes that have emerged from the previous sections. "Now that it's all over and done ... Seasons will pass you by ... I get up, I get down." Three major chords conclude the journey, and suddenly – but wholly fittingly – we are back in the forest of sound where we started, as the sound landscape recedes (17:39–18:42). "In my beginning is my end", as T. S. Eliot puts it. In concert, and in the *Yessongs* (1973) live version of the piece, Squire adds a series of slow, haunting bass harmonics right at the end, simultaneously a point of arrival and one of departure.

This lengthy song/suite is by far the most complete (in the sense of whole, coherent) musical statement Yes has ever produced. Bill Bruford put it well to Tim Morse in 1994: "The thing about 'Close to the Edge' is the form, I think. The shape of it is perfect. It's a real little part of history and it fits on the side of an album [LP] perfectly." Indeed so, but Yes still had another side of vinyl to fill, and they managed to do so with two further gems. Rick Wakeman has appropriately described 'And You And I' as "a kind of mini-quintet-sonata". Another Yes classic, it combines a pastoral feel with the real weight of an orchestral scale climax, first accentuated in the middle of the song, and then at the end. In concert it is given an epic feel through the use of earth-shattering bass pedals. Yet you have to remind yourself that it is, in fact, essentially a simple and quiet piece of music, introduced by Steve Howe's guitar harmonics (through to 1:11) in the easiest and most casual way. You can even hear him mouthing "OK" a couple of seconds in, as if to tell his fellow musicians that they are off and going. Then the six-note (4 and 2) drum and bass figure sounds, and we really are off. Howe's acoustic takes up the rhythm while Wakeman's Moog introduces the melody with great delicacy. Anderson enters with the opening vocal line at 1:39. The lyric is, once again, a word painting.

The songwriter has said that it is almost like a hymn, "but not in a church way" – an invocation that someone is there alongside us. A human companion, for sure. Possibly God. There is longing, ambiguity, anticipation, hope and a striving for presence. But it is also a given, it seems. The instrumental sections, 'Eclipse,' in the middle (3:43–5:45), and 'Apocalypse', at the end (8:33–9:22), were written by Squire and feature his bass applications. In between Howe's acoustic guitar and strumming return, pinpointed by Moog, to introduce the second wave of verse and chorus. "Political ends, as sad remains, will die / Reach out as forward tastes begin to enter you," Anderson sings. "All complete in the sight of seeds of life with you." After the dramatic instrumental finale, there is a gentle reprise: "And you and I called over valleys of endless seas…". As the words tail off, Howe's high steel guitar note bends upwards into the stratosphere and away into the heavens, carrying us to who know where. Wakeman sums 'And You and I' up in this way, in one of his interviews for the *Yes Years* documentary (1991):

> It has different movements which all go into each other. The object was of having a piece of music that was everything that the Yes critics hated us for and the Yes fans loved us for, which was emotion.

By contrast to the heavenly aesthetic preceding it, the final track on the album, the pulsing 'Siberian Khatru' (8'55"), is driving and earthbound. "We got lucky on that one", reckons Bill Bruford. The song is instrumentally driven in 5/4, with bass and drums locking and grooving together in a bar of eight and then a bar of seven. Following the urgent opening notes, Howe's guitar wails and winds throughout, while Wakeman adds a standout harpsichord solo (3:15–3:31) Meanwhile, no-one has ever fully figured out what a "khatru" is. A bird, Anderson has suggested. None has been seen of late in Siberia! The lyric centres on pairs of words and phrases that put together contrasting images, ideas, junctures and possibilities (5:29–6:18). The field of meaning is virtually endless, and dragged down only by fruitless or naïve attempts to pin it down.

"When you sing it, it feels right and makes sense ... but then you realise that you really don't know where it is these words are taking you. Also, the emotional span feels different each time." That's how one vocalist who has performed 'Siberian Khatru', and sung along with it, put it to me. In instrumental terms the song has a rawness and energy that has been well suited to opening concerts, segueing in from the climax of Stravinsky's *Firebird* or from Britten's *Young Person's Guide to the Orchestra*, which Yes have most frequently used as their introductory music – and which feel as much part of the catalogue to some as the notes they have produced themselves. Right at the end some ferocious scat singing (7:00–7:32) provides an interlude and raw cushion just ahead of the concluding guitar workout, enthusiastically joined by the other musicians. On the record, the song fades to distance (just one too many arguments to resolve there, maybe), though in concert it is given a not wholly satisfactory punchy ending. There was more to be said musically at this point, the listener may feel; but leaving it unsaid is suitably tantalising and somehow an appropriate way to end a breathtaking album.

In his essay 'Progressive Rock, "Close to the Edge", and the Boundaries of Style' (in *Understanding Rock: Essays in Musical Analysis*), scholar John Covach offers a quite sophisticated structural account of the title track of this album, elucidating the classical inferences and techniques employed, and examining the structures used and created to hold it all together. Romano also looks at the architecture of 'And You and I'. There have been several other attempts to render or explain what Yes are doing on *Close to the Edge* in terms of a classical form. Undoubtedly Wakeman, in particular, and later Moraz and

Khoroshev, brought these elements to the group. But I am not convinced that it is the best line of approach in trying to listen. In 1972 the band seemed to have an innate (though very hard struggled for) sense of form and style in the way they created the three quite different pieces on the album, and their component parts. But it was, to a significant extent, very much a 'make it up as you go along' enterprise. So what I have done in taking us through these three pieces of music is more a journey of accompaniment, noting features of the landscape, surprises, colours, textures and possible meanings as we proceed. It is one approach (but clearly not the only one) to surfacing the riches in, around and between the notes. In the end it is down to the listener to guide herself or himself. Words can but signpost.

Reconsidering the album in a wider context

Close to the Edge is a true musical landmark, the like of which will probably never be seen again. Is it art (a work to be appreciated in depth for its beauty and emotional or intellectual range)? Yes it is, and also rock (music designed to energise and empower at a visceral level). The two can and do overlap and go together. They don't have to, but they can, whatever Lester Bangs may think. At the time of the album's release, *Billboard* magazine (7 October 1972) singled it out for praise. The band, the reviewer suggested, had:

> progressed to the point where they are light years beyond their emulators, proving to be no mere flash in the pan. The sound tapestries they weave are dainty fragments, glimpses of destinies yet to be formed, times that fade like dew drops in the blurriness of desires half-remembered ... transcending the medium, it brings all senses into play.

Reception at the time veered from the laudatory to the highly puzzled, with Ian Macdonald feeling that the group were "not just close to the edge, they've gone right over it." *Close to the Edge* has received quite a bit of critical appreciation in the many years that have since elapsed – perhaps the last Yes album of its kind (determinedly 'progressive') to achieve that before the knives started to come out for and after *Tales From Topographic Oceans*.

Taking the longer view, *Close to the Edge* can be used as supporting evidence for Chris Squire's one-time claim, in the accompanying notes for the *YesYears* box set (1991), that Yes "never set out to feed the pop machine". That was certainly true for the accomplishments of the 1970s, though as I shall point out when we consider the output of the *90125* band, from the 1980s onwards there were more than a few working breakfasts, late lunches and evenings when they were found snacking at fast food restaurants! For even at their most adventurous, Yes (or at least those surrounding, supervising and advising the group) always had an ear for the market – and after the late 1970s that came to be a decidedly mixed blessing, as Steve Howe acknowledged in an interview connected with the band's 2011 recording, *Fly From Here*. But in 1972 the Yes barometer was set firmly towards uncharted waters, as the album that many regard as their definitive statement illustrates. That said, and as we have noted in passing, as soon as the lengthy recording process that gave birth to *Close to the Edge* was complete, drummer Bill Bruford swiftly packed his bags for the musical traveller's leap into King Crimson, an altogether murkier, more left-field "playing band", as he put it in his instructional video/DVD, *Bruford and the Beat* (1982).

To look towards the frontiers at that time was to encounter the likes of Soft Machine, Mahavishnu Orchestra and, of course, Crimson. Peter Banks says that these were the groups that forced Yes to rethink their strategy on several occasions in the journey from formation in late 1968 towards approaching maturity. Yes aspired to be in the same orbit as these pioneers, of course. But, as Bruford suggests, they were also in the business of offering, in the midst of comparative instrumental complexity (for a mainstream rock band), "a vocal entertainment". And that, from his point of view, meant both that *Close to the Edge* was the apex of what Yes could achieve within the parameters fixed by conventional vocal harmony, and concomitantly that the capacity for genuine improvisation and minor key experimentation was going to be limited – certainly compared with the likes of second-stage Crimson and all that they portended.

Bruford commented more recently (2011):

> Had I been less curious I would have stayed with Yes. [...] Neither Yes nor Crimson, while having considerable attributes of their own, were ever going to be the free-wheeling, loose jazz-ish groups that I wanted to be in but didn't really know I wanted to be in. [It] took me a while to get there.

The mid-'80s, in fact, by which time Yes were improbably reformed and touring large stadia and aircraft hangars with a seven plus-million selling hit album and a number one R&B chart single. How strange is musical life. All that at least puts into perspective the destiny of the 'progressive' attributes credited to Yes and others in the early '70s, or the equally flawed claims by Lester Bangs and his lesser acolytes that they were somehow "non-rock".

Nonetheless, the band's achievement on *Close to the Edge* was considerable (as Bruford, among others who remain sceptical within and beyond the 'prog' fold, has acknowledged). The album, given a fresh gleam by the definitive Wilson 5.1 rendition, continues to hold up incredibly strongly when listened to some 45 plus years after its creation. This alone suggests that it possesses merits greater than being natively 'popular' in certain circles, and indicates that its non-standard hybridity can still provide the necessary aural hooks for a (post)modern audience to grasp its virtues. In 1972 the album was undoubtedly what could have been termed 'progressive'. These days, when progress is not quite what it used to be in music, I would place it more in the arena of 'rock-based art fusion' ('out-rock' rather than 'post-rock'), a form of musical typology I will refer to again in Chapter 14.

So where does that leave us at this point in the band's musical journey? There is a respectable argument to be made that the members of Yes would have been better going their separate ways after *Close to the Edge,* leaving the group to bow out on an undeniable high note after two promising and three highly acclaimed ones. That way, the band's reputation would be unsullied, iconic even. Sighs of 'what might have been' are certainly much more likely to build an ensemble's reputation than moans of 'they've lost it' or 'they could never reach that pinnacle again' for many years to come. Likewise, it could be said that little that the band has done since their 1972 masterpiece could lay claim to the kind of originality that this record embodied in its time and moment, and as an enduring musical artefact.

I suspect that case could be well argued by Bruford, who left at exactly the right time for his own career, though to the continuing puzzlement of those who do not share his artistic ethic and outlook. That said, he would perhaps also admit to having heard little of what Yes has done since (apart from a brief vacation with the band for the *Union* tour). Others would also want to suggest that there have been more than enough highs since *Close to the Edge* to make the often tortuous 45 plus years since then worthwhile for a very large number of people. In particular, I shall argue, *Tales From Topographic Oceans* and *Relayer,* plus 'Awaken', deserve just as much praise in their own way as *Edge* – even if they have faced far more critical questions. So should 1977 then have been 'the End', musically and artistically? Is the Yes deeply forged by *Close to the Edge* an artefact from a past era that has outlived its usefulness? We will cross that critical bridge, too, when we get to it – and to the very different set of Yeses that launched themselves into the world in the 1980s.

Chapter 5
High the Memory (*Tales From Topographic Oceans*)

As one with the knowledge and magic of the source
Attuned to the majesty of music
They marched as one with the Earth.

– Yes, 'The Ancient'

By far the most controversial music Yes has ever recorded lies on the ambitiously extended, four-part conceptual album, *Tales From Topographic Oceans*, released in Europe in December 1973 and in North America a month later. Yes toured the more than eighty minutes of music it contains from November 1973 to April 1974, with a set that featured the work in its entirety. This was initially before the LP had been released, and therefore before its contents had been heard by most of the intended audience. It was an extraordinarily bold and courageous move to make. Yes subsequently dropped sides two and three from their concert list, concentrating on the more approachable side one and side four, which have endured in the repertoire ever since. The album was reissued in 1994 and incorporated in tours from 1996 to 1998 and from 2000 to 2002. Then it was remastered with bonus tracks in 2003. It reappeared in live performance in 2004 and again from 2016 to 2018, the band's fiftieth anniversary year. An edition with new stereo and 5.1 surround sound mixes by Steven Wilson, including additional material, was released in October 2016, to some acclaim among the album's advocates.

While it proved a commercial success in its early years, partly driven by huge pre-sales secured on the back of the critical and popular acclaim achieved by *Close to the Edge*, the band's longest-ever work tended to bewilder critics and audiences alike. Some hailed it as a musical breakthrough. It certainly was for me, and remains among the pinnacles of the band's musical achievements (if not its highest peak) for many others. Devoted journalistic supporters of the group have also stood by *Tales* over the years, despite doubts. Music writer Chris Welch, though partly agnostic, once described it as "a fragmented masterpiece". But the overall verdict within the rock world has been predominantly condemnatory, with *Tales* being variously traduced as 'unwieldy', 'pretentious', 'wishy-washy', 'incoherent', 'padded to death', 'psychedelic doodling' and 'grandiloquently vacuous'. Even Yes's then keyboard player, the famously flamboyant (but musically conservative) Rick Wakeman, who had helped create it, enthusiastically joined these public denunciations – though he drew back from at least some of them subsequently and accommodated with the band to perform side one, 'The Revealing Science of God', 25 times on the 2002 US tour, and side four, 'Ritual', a further 34 times on the 2004 tour.

The album's rejection seems to have become yet another foregone conclusion for generations of commentators who appear barely to have given it a moment's ear space, let alone serious attention – as with Jimmy Guterman in *The Worst Rock 'n Roll*

Records of All Time (Citadel, 1991), for example. That should at least give us cause to question the ease of condemnation. Partly because of the curious combination of venom and bafflement the album has elicited, compounded by broader antagonistic attititudes towards progressive rock (whose chief sins it is supposed, archetypally, to embody), it is very difficult to approach *Tales* without heavily weighted presuppositions and prejudices. I certainly cannot pretend not to do so because, as I indicated above, and in the opening Chapter of this book, it was the album which, more than any other (and subsequently in tandem with *Close to the Edge* and *Relayer*) bred in me a deep and abiding love for the music of Yes. What follows is therefore a case for a positive – though not uncritical – appraisal of the album, starting with an overview of the category problems that rapidly emerge in any attempt to offer an assessment of it.

Tales of change within the sound

Much of the critical opprobrium faced by *Tales From Topographic Oceans* derives from strong, received feelings about what constitutes 'authenticity' in rock music – it should be something visceral, straightforward, accessible, popular and, in most cases, danceable, claim the purists. There is a corresponding sense that musicians working in the rock sphere are automatically overreaching their mandate or competence when they seek to incorporate, expand on, or allude to more expressive musical ideas from a range of other influences. This is the "overbearing pretentiousness" that Ernesto Lechner and others have frequently alleged with regard to Yes during this period of their creative output. Given this style of responding to the music, eclecticism soon gets conflated with a pejoratively perceived mongrelism. Similarly, extended form without any defined precedent is readily confused with shapelessness, while reflective musical interludes are seen merely as 'padding' – Rick Wakeman's constant refrain about *Tales*. Some of these issues can be fairly readily addressed and rejected at the level of formal analysis. The album may have an eccentric and unconventional structure, for example; but structure there most certainly is. Other concerns inevitably remain matters of taste rooted in cultural practice that no amount of argument is ever likely to resolve. Nevertheless, they also invite alternative experiences and perceptions, not in order to quash the challengers (everyone is entitled to their musical preferences), but rather to relocate reception of the album in a wider range of musical possibilities.

If there is a paradox (or perhaps a series of paradoxes) built into *Tales From Topographic Oceans,* maybe a key to understanding it lies in the title, and in the artwork supplied by Roger Dean. Oceans have layers, but no topography. Topographic features are structured rather than watery. Yet Yes have attempted to bring the two together and render them part of our common musical experience. Equally, the landscaping that Dean created to adorn the album contains most of the features you would readily expect – earth, sky and sea – but presented and adorned in unexpected ways. There are many moons and symbols. Past and future seem to flow into one another. There is the Mayan temple at Chichen Itza with the sun behind it (specifically requested by Jon Anderson). There are features of English landscape: Brimham Rocks at the edge of Land's End, the Logan Rock at Treen, and single stones from Avebury and Stonehenge. There are fish and stars; a sky that is the sea and vice versa. The whole coheres wonderfully, teasing the imagination into action. Yet the individual features remain disparate and far-flung in time and in space.

Inside the album we also discover a series of openings onto the world (as if viewed from curved aircraft windows) interspersed with the highly figurative, extensive and metaphorical lyrics. Somehow, all this comes across as a metaphor for the album as a whole, and an indication as to what to anticipate – both the expected and the wholly unexpected – as the notes within it unfold and create their own intriguing world. Interestingly, despite the magazine's general aversion to Yes (and to *Tales*), the readers of *Rolling Stone* voted the album's illustration as the best cover art of all time in 2002. It is certainly among the most unusual, and among the best of Dean's work – which itself has had a mixed reception over the years. Guitarist and co-composer Steve Howe sums it up well, in a short video interview sequence for the 2017 live album, *Topographic Drama*, which reprises two sides of *Tales* live from 2016, as well as other material. The aim of the artwork and the album together is "to be elaborate, to be detailed and to be beautiful", he says, "and I do think that music should be beautiful".

So what of the four pieces of music that comprise the album themselves? That awkward descriptor 'pieces' to denote the four units of *Tales* indicates an immediate difficulty. What language shall we borrow or generate to talk about this 83-minute musical creation and its component parts? In the vinyl era, there was an obvious way out of this dilemma. The whole edifice was both produced and heard as four 'sides' across two records, each limited to a maximum of 22 minutes. In the CD era they became 'tracks'. But the question remains: what is the actual relationship within and between these different pieces of music? Some have used the nineteenth and twentieth century instrumental term 'movements' to describe them. Others have spoken of them as 'songs'. The former, though possibly closer to the reality, risks imposing a European 'classical' frame (as if that was automatically appropriate, and as if it meant just one thing). The latter presupposes the fixity of rock in terms of a consecutive series of mainly vocal entertainments. Neither gives a real indicator as to what is happening in this music, or with this album.

Tales From Topographic Oceans arose from a unifying field of vision, created particularly from the compositional (lyrical-musical) collaboration of Jon Anderson and Steve Howe. It drew upon a pretty loose interpretation of the four-part *shastras* (precepts, rules, manual and compendium) arising in different areas of Hindu thought and referred to in a lengthy footnote in Paramahansa Yogananda's *Autobiography of a Yogi* (1946). But it also originated – more prosaically – in a laborious process of construction, editing, arranging, producing and engineering over a period of five months in the studio. The final structure and content of *Tales,* necessarily divided in terms of the constraints imposed by the recorded music vehicle of the day, the long-playing record, therefore contains continuities and discontinuities, innovations and reappraisals, across its four stand-alone – but also interlocking – musical segments. These consonances and variations only become evident through repeated listening to the development of the whole album. Some of them are clearly intentional. Others may be coincidental. Both compositional intent and listener response must contribute to any emerging musical narrative by which we may "reach out and touch the sound".

As with *Close to the Edge,* which I examined in the last Chapter, there have been various attempts to suggest that *Tales From Topographic Oceans* conforms, in some broad sense, to the sonata form that evolved in Western art music from the eighteen century onwards. As in other cases involving the music of Yes, these attempts ultimately fail at a technical and procedural level, in my view. In so doing they provoke more questions than answers, though the questions may be interesting ones in their own right. In short, there is just too much thematic and tonal unevenness at play in this 'album' (again, note that this is the pragmatic product-term we find ourselves falling back onto, rather than 'symphony' or 'tone poem') to subsume it under any one received musical mode. Nevertheless, there is initiation, variation, development, recapitulation and resolution within each of the four units, as well as within the whole. That is what makes it, at once, so singular and so multifaceted.

Understandably, it is the different (even contradictory) dimensions of the musical whole – rather than its common threads – that first impress themselves upon the listener, before greater familiarity begins to cohere into a more connected, encompassing experience. For example, on the first side alone, we are confronted with found sounds, hauntingly metrical chanting, an Arabesque guitar figure, verses and choruses, contrapuntal washes of sound texture in competing time signatures, a fast and violent stab of keyboards, a simple but interrupted drum pattern, ascending and descending clusters of notes, climactic dynamics, and more. Whatever this is, it is not conventional 'classical' instrumentation. But nor is it crowd-pleasing music theatre orchestration, simple song-smithery, 'world' music, 'jazz-rock fusion' or postmodern pastiche – some of which pre-dated and some of which post-dated the arrival of the album.

Overall, *Tales* is most definitely Western music (until we get to Eastern intonations in elements of side three, 'The Ancient'). It is tonal but with shifting tone centres, breezily diatonic with questioning undertones and a minor key resolution, metrically regular but with changes and sudden variations, richly coloured in a way that sometimes clarifies and sometimes obscures the five basic instrumental components, anthemic in parts, and occasionally discordant. It is rendered whole by a clear and constant (though shifting) relationship between guitars, bass, vocals, drums/percussion and keyboards, all of which can be picked out and identified on their own as well as in their blending. This is most evident on Wilson's 5.1 mixes.

The album as a whole is heavily emotionally flavoured in its construction, development and impact. There are numerous themes and melodies. Some of these are extended and morphed, others virtually thrown away. There are recurrences and non-recurrences of both harmonic and lyrical material ... and so it goes on. No wonder the fans and the critics were initially confused. *Close to the Edge* had pointed in this direction, but its form and structure was rather more identifiable, as Bill Bruford and others have pointed out. *Close to the Edge* was also shorter and there were two distinct songs alongside one extended piece. It was altogether more manageable.

By contrast, *Tales* takes on an extended, malleable shape across its entire length. Its structure is a unique one, devised section by section, to allow the different musical components to shine through while fitting together. It clearly arises from rock textures, but consciously blends together a far wider range of influences. It pushes forward accessible melodies and harmonies, while also taking the occasional holiday from them. It ebbs and flows, transporting the listener through a lengthy musical journey with little direct, obvious or advanced mapping. Each of the four sides is structured differently, according to their own needs. The whole album reaches a conclusion that is both firm (two huge, contrasting climaxes, one distinctly rhythmic and the other melodically and harmonically integrating, on 'Ritual') and also floating (the final wispy, receding thirty seconds). It rests its musical case overall not just upon on loud assertion, but upon emotionally charged dynamic contrasts, different textures, and shorter, quiet, questioning, almost idyllic passages. What follows is not a narrating of all four sides and a structural account of them (you can find that in some detail in Thomas Mosbø's, *Yes: But What Does It Mean?* Wyndstar, 1994). Rather, it is an attempt to point out some key features of the musical landscape, in sequence. And then to leave the listener to explore for her or himself.

The Revealing Science of God (Dance of the Dawn)
When *Tales* was digitally re-mastered by Joe Gastwirt at Ocean View for a 2003 release (with two additional studio run-throughs) to mark its thirtieth anniversary, the original beginning of the album's first movement, 'The Revealing Science of God', was finally restored – rendering it 22' 22" long, rather

than 20' 25". That introductory 1:57 instrumental, excluded from the original vinyl LP only because it would not fit without compromising overall sound quality, begins with the tidal roar of the sea, increasing in pace and dynamics. Then Steve Howe's pleading steel guitar makes an appearance, introducing the initial notes of the first theme, augmented by gentle but firm organ swells. These grow into an oboe-like synth effect, leading to a partial crescendo, before Jon Anderson comes in with first line of the opening choral section. There is a parallel with *Close to the Edge,* which also emerges from layers of natural sound, but the effect is much more like a siren across the water rather than the buzz of a forest and the crash of a waterfall.

The chanted opening verse (1:57, "Dawn of Light"), in B natural, is foundational to the whole piece, with Anderson's choir-boy northern English burr introducing recurring rich harmonies, backed by wailing synth and cymbal splashes. The climax is a deep bass and synth chord (3:30) that opens up a summery keyboard flourish topped by Howe's gorgeous guitar figure (3:55–4:07). This is repeated and adapted on keys, accompanied by bass and drums, and then built by the whole band (4.28). It is sumptuous and panoramic in its feel. A hint of sonar, occurring throughout, comes in at 4:53, before Anderson returns with his next vocal theme (5:02, "Talk to the sunlight caller"). The main chorus ("What happened to this song we once knew so well?') appears at 6:02. Steve Howe once somewhat jocularly remarked that:

> Side one was the commercial or easy-listening side of *Topographic Oceans,* side two was a much lighter, folky side of Yes, side three was electronic mayhem turning into acoustic simplicity, and side four was us trying to drive the whole thing home. (Chambers, 2002, page 31).

It stretches the musical imagination to describe 'The Revealing Science of God' as easy listening, but it has a more popular appeal melodically, and the chorus is probably the most settled and predictable line in the piece. With a further verse and chorus, the opening section of 'The Revealing' climaxes at 8:30 ("We must have waited all our lives for this moment"), before heading off in a new direction with a suddenly increased tempo and a quite different mood (8:49).

Burbling synth and bass and an insistent rhythm then prefigure the "star light movements" theme, with its crystalline vocal delivery. At 9:43 we are suddenly brought down with a diminuendo into a quiet, loose-limbed interlude led by White and Howe. This is possibly one of the elements of *Tales* regarded as 'padding' by Wakeman and others. On the contrary, for me it works beautifully, relieving the growing intensity of the music and reflecting the ebb and flow of the topographic ocean we are at times riding, at times being carried by, at times submerged under – and at times (like this) floating with. The Mellotron adds a gorgeous orchestral texture at 11:00, with Howe's guitar providing relaxed, finely picked counterpoint melody. They are playing at the same time and at different times, creating a sense of going against the tide and the current. This is surely one of the most effective moments of the whole piece. Anderson re-enters with a poignant observation ("I just can't believe our song will leave you") at 11:42, heightened by the glorious interlacing of keys and guitar, before the drums, bass and piano (13:07) introduce a rather different, conflicting chant from the opening one ("Skyline teacher / warland seeker / send out poison") at 13:13. Squire's bass thunders in at 13:46, interrupting the tempo and darkening the mood, before Howe suddenly warps the clean, accompanying guitar line into an alternating, frenzied *dance macabre*. At 14:46 we are back in calmer instrumental waters, with a repeated acoustic theme backed by tuned percussion and (15:30) the return of the Mellotron (15:55).

Anderson's "And through the rhythm of moving slowly" section is backed by an angular, irregular tempo leading up to the return of the previous instrumental and vocal theme from 9:43

onwards. This time, however, it is mediated (18:00) by a powerful vocal and instrumental climax, leading into a fabulously fast, aggressive, wailing and ornamented mini-Moog solo from Wakeman (18:37–19:26) backed by the whole band in 6/8. It is a moment of pulsing adrenalin and high drama. Then suddenly the tension evaporates into a modulated orchestral wash, and Anderson returns with a vocal line of heart-breaking intensity (19:37, "they move fast, they tell me…", building towards "a course towards a universal season"). We are now approaching the *dénouement*, as the previously stated vocal and instrumental themes come together (20:36), recapitulated towards a climax (20:55, "what happened to this song…"). The refrain "we must have waited all our lives" is harmonised and layered, and then the quiet, filigree vocal ending takes over (21:40–22:44), resolving from B natural to the dominant E major. It is a moment of incredible beauty and emotional subtlety, amplified by the way that the instruments lend delicacy and colour to the shifting dynamics.

Key features throughout 'The Revealing Science of God' include Howe's signature Gibson ES-175 guitar lines. The original material was supposedly 28 minutes long, but six minutes were shaved off to ensure that it fitted on one side of vinyl. The "Young Christians see it" section (15:55–17:16) originated from a take recorded during the *Fragile* recording sessions. This earlier material was previously unreleased until the album's 2015 reissue, which contained the track named 'All Fighters Past'. It works far better, in my view, with the counter-rhythm and slower pace on *Tales*. Steve Howe, incidentally, plays a Danelectro guitar, a lute and a Martin acoustic at various places on the track.

The Remembering (High the memory)

Side two of the album starts off in a quite different vein and mode, with a quirky little synth and guitar line, alternating with an echoing riff that recurs throughout the side. The nautical feel on the sound world of what is effectively a more pastoral piece of music is established from the outset. The major themes and shifts are carried primarily by Wakeman's textured keyboards (with some parts created by White, apparently), which are quite a contrast to his usual fast, quasi-Baroque and highly ornamented approach.

Chris Squire's tuneful Guild fretless bass is also an important feature throughout, playing a significant role in the gentle construction of the punctuated opening verse (0:38–2:28, "As the silence of seasons on…"), which gives rise to a second vocal theme ("Ours, the story shall we carry on") at 2:33. It picks up the "they move fast" lyric from 'The Revealing', heightened through to 4:26 and onto a marvellous 'suspended time' Mellotron interlude (4:35). Again, this is among Wakeman's finest pieces of work with the band, recurring later on 'The Remembering'.

The folk feel, reinforced with some nevertheless pretty adventurous arrangement and instrumentation, gives way to a stronger pulse, as bass and drums kick in at 5:41. The Mellotron is back forcefully at 3:38, in a passage that proved difficult to replicate live because of the unreliability of the instrument. At 8:11 the MiniMoog intrudes a new lead line, and Squire's intense phrasing gives way to Howe's acoustic as the pace and mood changes suddenly into the "Don the cap…" section, with the bass beautifully enhancing and complementing the sustained melodic figure on the guitar, especially from 10:23–10:38, before the song returns with an even more punchy instrumental foundation.

At 11:14 Wakeman's keyboards once again effect a transition to a more delicate, initially acoustic song reprise ("Other Skylines to hold you") before the gutsy "relayer" section (13:08–13:45). Squire's ferocious bass and White's drums anchor a fiery synth line from 13:56 until Anderson breaks in with, "Stand on hills of long forgotten yesterdays / Pass amongst your memories told returning ways". It is the beginning of what will be a climactic finale. At 15:50 Wakeman appears with his most nautically charged synth imagery to date, full of depth and body. It is an absolutely remarkable piece of sound painting, joined by Squire at 17:06 to add pressure. Then at 17:35 the instrumental forces combine to launch us into what is possibly one of the most intense finales (especially from 18:52) in the history of Yes music, resolving itself in a powerful instrumental coda (19:26) in which Howe's guitar is axial. Once again, however, the band uses tension and release to land another extraordinary piece of music in exactly the right place, taking the foot off the accelerator at 19:47 to reinstate a drifting calm right at the end (20:34). Jon Anderson told *Beat* magazine in 1974:

> The whole band got involved in playing like the sea – rhythms, eddies, swells and undercurrents – while we were doing it.

The Ancient (Giants Under the Sun)

Jon Anderson's original liner notes capture the dramatic shift of mood, instrumentation and feel as a massive, shuddering gong and crashing cymbals (00:01–00:30) introduce 'The Ancient'. He writes that this piece of music:

> probes still further into the past beyond the point of remembering. Here Steve [Howe]'s guitar is pivotal in sharpening reflection on the beauties and treasures of lost civilisations, Indian, Chinese, Central American, Atlantean. These and other people left an immense treasure of knowledge.

Note, in passing, the casual treatment of Atlantis as other than a fictional island mentioned within an allegory on the hubris of nations in Plato's works, *Timaeus* and *Critias*. Anderson makes a similar reference to Atlantis, alongside historical civilisations, in 'The Calling', on the very different 1994 album, *Talk*.

Alongside parts of the *Relayer* album (1974), 'The Ancient' is possibly the most adventurous and wildly freeform sounding piece of music Yes ever created. "I think it's too much for most people," Chris Squire ventured to Tim Morse in 1994. The piece revolves substantially around ideas formed, shaped and delivered by Howe's telescopic guitar explorations. He had been struck, it seems, by the hypnotic effect on audiences of Frank Zappa's extended guitar solos, and wanted to find out what he could achieve with his own style and ambition in a rather different musical context. His solos on the third side of *Tales From Topographic Oceans* are very carefully crafted, despite their free association feel, and also have a distinctly 'live' ambience to them. Howe plays a steel guitar and a Spanish Ramirez acoustic on the track, and gave producer Eddy Offord several recordings by classical guitarist Julian Bream as a guide to the kind of sound he wanted in the acoustic sections. In 1991 I was fortunate enough to have an hour-long interview with the guitarist, around the time of the release of his solo album, *Turbulence*. We talked about 'Ritual', side four of *Tales,* but one of my regrets is that we didn't manage to delve further into 'The Ancient', which had been my intention. I somehow got waylaid from my questioning in what was otherwise a fascinating conversation about Howe's musical influences and pathways.

Alan White's drums and assorted percussion are also crucial to the construction and sound world of the third side of *Tales* – not least its restless energy, primal power and complex light and shade. The instrumental playing throughout is very strong. Yes are at the height of their powers on this album and the ones that immediately precede and follow it. White uses bells, in addition to a gong, cymbals and tuned percussion. Howe's melodic ideas are demonstrative and austere. Harmony is virtually abandoned in the pursuit of a tone that is at once visceral and reflective, rounding off into glissandos early on, and using sustain to real effect. Squire's bass, meanwhile, moves away from melody and more towards rhythm again in this track.

Each side of *Tales* sounds remarkably different (one and four perhaps having most in common), while showcasing different facets of the musicians, both on their own and in multiple combinations. Wakeman makes a transitional appearance at 3:16, and at 3:40 bass and drums reintroduce the theme from the prelude, augmented by rising chords on guitar and keyboards, and an octave leap on bass. It is powerful and evocative playing. The first element of song, brief and lingering, comes in at 4:15, consisting entirely of the recitation cited at the beginning of this Chapter. Then we are back to Howe's guitar, and a series of passages in which, at one point, synth and guitar swap phrases in 7/8. In the middle there is another short chant sequence, involving several translations of the word "sun", or phases associated with the sun, in a variety of languages and word sounds dreamt up by Anderson. Howe continues to use repetitions, variations and ascending chains of notes in his soloing, introducing and reintroducing key thematic material at just after 10 and 12 minutes.

At 12:25 there is a major and unexpected shift in the piece, as the acoustic guitar breaks in to calm the storm and to move the music from an electric tone reminiscent of Eastern scales and harmonies, towards a non-electric one evoking a classical sensibility. At first he is accompanying Jon Anderson: "So the flowering creativity of life wove its web". We are moved lyrically from one frame of musical reference to another. Then at 12:49 the solo proper begins. It is a finely wrought piece, seemingly done 'as live' in the studio. At 14:37 there is another shift, this time into 'Leaves of Green', the only song proper in 'The Ancient', and one possessing a disarming simplicity, almost a naïvety. The acoustic guitar sequence and song have often been performed, both by Howe solo and as part of Yes, as stand-alone features. One of the repeated electric guitar themes re-enters from 17:44 to 18:05 to effect a final resolution to the extended puzzle that is

'The Ancient' ... but only to be usurped by four crashing pairs of notes and an ascending synth and steel guitar scale through to 18:33. It is as if we are suspended in mid air, waiting for what is to come.

Ritual (Nous Sommes du Soleil)

The opening of 'Ritual' leaves you in little doubt that the fourth side of *Tales* is to be a grand finale in its own right, though one that itself goes through both yearningly romantic and hauntingly violent phases. In addition to the studio original and remixes, there is a very good live rendition on the *Yesshows* album (1977) and on *Yes: Symphonic Live* (2002). Many still believe the recorded best live version is from Roosevelt Stadium, NJ, USA in 1976, but that has never been officially released.

The piece begins with an 18-second declamatory, staccato instrumental theme carried by bass and drums with keyboard and guitars, before Steve Howe's Gibson pivots us into the stratosphere with a life-affirming figure that also hints back to 'The Remembering' and will form the basis of the final coda. White's drums punch out an accompaniment and Squire's bass joins the melody at the top end, before Wakeman enters with a circular figure at 00:48. Bass marks time until the drums reintroduce the guitar at 1:03 for a major restatement of the second theme. At 1:31 a descending and ascending bass riff, backed by swirling keys, signals the next instrumental focus, initially accompanied by Anderson's vocal harmonising. The beat is syncopated, there are moments when synth comes to the fore, then harmony vocals, guitar, keys again, then bass and drums, combining and swapping the material and building it to an energising, dance-like level, swaying us into the feel of the ritual to which the track title refers.

Chris Squire's bass, backed by vocal harmony, breaks in decisively at 3:41, having the final say with a descending and ascending motif before a final crash (3:57) and some orchestral synth takes us down into a murkier, less certain instrumental space. Out of the gathering darkness emerges Steve Howe's guitar (4:09), pinpointing the light again with a beautifully elaborated melodic idea that rises and soars above the percussive maelstrom, referencing 'The Revealing'. There's also a mini-allusion to 'Close to the Edge' thrown in for good measure. The threads of *Tales* and its antecedents are slowly but surely being drawn together. At 5:15 the "Nous Sommes du Soleil" theme is foregrounded on guitar, the Mellotron surges momentarily, and Jon Anderson's bell-like vocals begin (5:28). The chorus sequence has a jazzy feel to it, while Howe's guitar sings its own tune, and Wakeman's keyboards conjure up the lush orchestral backdrop. It is jaw-droppingly beautiful.

Finally the opening verse ("Open doors we find our way / We look, we see, we smile / Surely daybreaks cross our path / And stay maybe a while") arrives at 6:48. The song builds, grows, swells and develops through to the bass picking up the theme ("at all...") in double time at 10:45 towards a climax at 11:10. A Squire pitch-bend with splashes of drums rounding it off acts as a bridge to the driving, percussive six-minute central instrumental section, led on bass, which commences at 12:09. This section goes through four phases, with Squire's majestic, energised playing propelling it forward before Wakeman (13:26) raises it further and Howe returns (13: 37) with a triumphant tone to elevate the theme to yet another level. At 14:20 White breaks the life force apart, with bells and assorted percussion announcing what is often referred to as 'the battle sequence'. In concert, it has involved not just the drummer but also other members of the band joining in on percussion pads and kettledrums. The cacophony is almost overpowering, at one point mimicking and parodying Howe's early Arabesque figure in 'The Revealing'. In so doing it embodies the forces of death ranged against those of life and affirmation.

Deranged wailing synth sounds anticipate what will later be another titanic struggle at the heart of 'The Gates of Delirium' on *Relayer*. The hissing, thundering noise is finally ended by Steve Howe's guitar, re-announcing an earlier joyous theme, segueing (17:21) into the song of love that lies at the core of 'Ritual', once all the sound and fury has dissipated. "Hold me my love, hold me today, call me round ... We love when we play" sings Anderson, with some groundwork piano initially provided by White. The song of innocence emerges out of the tumult of experience. Bill Martin (*Music of Yes: Structure and Vision in Progressive Rock*, 1996) detects what may be a subconscious Blakean Romanticism within the music of Yes. This is certainly one of the places where this can be seen.

But we are not done yet. At 19:46 the vocal ends, there is a change of key, and an instrumental *tour de force* draws the track towards a close. The coda (19:51 onwards) is group playing, but it is led by guitar. Thomas Mosbø (1994) writes:

> The depth and pathos communicated through Howe's guitar in this final passage is incredible, carrying with it the entire content of the spiritual journey of *Tales*.

The last word (21:01) however, is in a long, drawn-out, breathy minor chord. It is a compelling end to a remarkable piece of music, and indeed a remarkable suite of lengthy elaborate pieces. A considerable achievement overall.

We advance, we retrace our story

In any attempt to describe or analyse *Tales From Topographic Oceans*, you find yourself, in my experience, reasoning with a mystery. The album is an 'ever opening flower'. Nothing substitutes for the notes, but the notes are such as to invite a response that goes beyond them. To describe the album as 'unwieldy', 'padded', 'incoherent' or 'grandiose' is to miss the subtlety, dexterity and determination with which such a large palette of musical resources is brought together, displayed and directed towards the aim of ... what, exactly? Aye, there's the rub. With a conventional 'rock song', there is usually an identifiable pay-off, in terms of a repeated hook, riff, dance sequence, line or pulse. Sometimes this is disguised or delayed, but often it achieves its impact by being obvious and emphasised. Yes has leaned in this direction on numerous occasions, too, especially from the 1980s onwards. With this album, however, we are on quite different territory. The familiar is segued into the experimental. Climaxes can be less than predictable or final. Identifiable 'songs' are weaved into a much more variable musical texture. In short, far, far more is expected or required of the listener over an extended period of time to get the most out of the music. It is possible to get to grips with one section, one 'side', two or three 'sides', and/or the whole work. Without going all the way, however, something is missing. This is inspiring and elevating music, but it also has a serious, transcendental quality. Chris Welch, who as we have observed has waxed and waned somewhat about the value of *Tales*, is not wrong to say that in its grooves there is a 'masterpiece' struggling to get out. But neither is he wrong to say that it lies in 'fragments'. However, these fragments are arranged, gathered, shaped and shared with passion and attention.

Lester Bangs once said that:

The first mistake of art is to assume that it's serious ... [whereas] the main reason we listen to music in the first place is to hear passion expressed.

However, why should there be any essential contradiction between seriousness and passion? Some of our passions are necessarily explosive, humorous and ephemeral, of course. There is nothing wrong with that. But it is equally no reason to deny deeper, more abiding passions sustained by thoughtfulness and by more developed languages (in music and elsewhere) capable of carrying a broader weight of experience and reflection; of offering further riches and many more surprises and insights over the years. *Tales From Topographic Oceans* is in that category for me. And while Yes has produced much more immediate and less weighty music, which I can also enjoy and value, the core of the band's lasting appeal lies, for some of us, in what will endure and entice when an assuredly well-crafted song like 'Owner of a Lonely Heart' has outlived its capacity for surprise after repeated listens. That is an aesthetic viewpoint that will not appeal to everyone. But no matter. Without music that pushes our boundaries and invites us into passions and possibilities we never really knew before we encountered it, we impoverish the rich vocabulary out of which all musical endeavours – from the purposefully dense to the joyfully frivolous – can draw.

Chapter 6
Electric Freedom
(Relayer)

From the moment I reached out to hold, I felt a sound
And what touches our soul slowly moves as touch rebounds

— Yes, 'Sound Chaser'

The very best Yes music always seems to be presaged by creative disruption and personnel changes. While the band's original line-up remained constant for the first two albums, the third breakthrough one (*The Yes Album*) required the arrival of Steve Howe on guitar to ignite it, while the fourth and fifth (*Fragile* and *Close to the Edge*) involved the explosive inspiration of keyboard entrepreneur and proto-celebrity, Rick Wakeman. After Bill Bruford's departure from the drum riser, Alan White came on board for the band's sixth outing, the monumental *Tales From Topographic Oceans*. He offered the weight and swing that proved just right to nail down what was undoubtedly a sprawling, variegated and hugely ambitious project.

However, the inner mounting turmoil was not to end there. Though he produced what I would argue was among his best work with Yes (or indeed for any other musical context) on *Tales*, Wakeman was not happy by the time the album emerged, and was even less happy during and after touring it. The record was not to his taste, the musical direction of the band was too exploratory and disconnected for him, and his rock'n'roll lifestyle and persona did not seem to gel at that time with a group that took itself and its music increasingly seriously. The keyboard showman quit the band at the end of the tour in May 1974 and headed off to further his growing solo career with the more theatrically styled and popular *Journey to the Centre of the Earth*.

This left Yes with the challenging task of finding a replacement behind the keys who could carry the weight of the kind of music they wanted to explore. Various people were tried out, including one Evángelos Odysséas Papathanassíou (better known as Vangelis). Finally, the band lit upon Swiss player, composer and arranger Patrick Moraz, fresh out of a band called Refugee. Moraz had studied classical music at the Lausanne Conservatory and had started his career in jazz. He had formed four bands himself already, and he had been involved in scoring a number of European art films. He also had some funk leanings and an interest in what later became dubbed 'world music', especially music from South America. His overall technique surpassed that of previous Yes keyboard players, he could marshal a battery of electronic instruments (as well as piano, harpsichord and pipe organ) and he was keen to be part of a band that could stretch him musically as well as utilising his considerable capabilities. The initial fit seemed really good, in spite of some obvious differences in culture and background. The new band member wanted to strengthen the experimental, jazz and electronic side of Yes, and that is exactly where they ended up heading for what turned out to be the only studio album the enigmatic Moraz would produce with the group: the bold, adventurous and (in some circles) controversial *Relayer*.

If involvement with *Tales From Topographic Oceans* had already proved a stretch too far for melodic, elaborate, song-oriented stylist Rick Wakeman, the metallic, dissonant and fusion-fired *Relayer* album was even further out of his orbit. It was full of what Tim Morse has neatly called hyperkinetic energy. It was jazzy and avant-garde. Wakeman has since said that it is a recording to which he simply cannot relate. When he heard and reviewed it, his conclusion was that he had been right to leave. But this music was exactly where Patrick Moraz was and where he wanted to be.

By the time I first heard *Relayer*, I was familiar with two Yes albums, *Tales* and *Close to the Edge*. Both had made an enormous impact on me. But *Relayer* knocked me sideways. It was something completely new for me, and took some listening to grow into. I knew almost instantly that it was exciting and different, but its musical language was still strange, haunting and aggressive. I had little experience of jazz at the time, and not much exposure to the world of fusion within which the album is perhaps most readily located – although its form and style, being more on the rock side of the jazz–rock spectrum, is still far from that of Miles Davis, Chick Corea, Mahavishnu Orchestra, Weather Report or any of the other leading exponents in that genre (which in its own way is as contested, misrepresented and reviled as its distant but not entirely remote cousin, progressive rock). At any event, while I struggled to understand *Relayer* at first, I knew instinctively that it would be important, life-changing even. Not just for me as listener, but for the band. In fact it turned out to be a terminus rather than a point of departure for Yes in the 1970s. Some of us still wonder what might have happened if the band had ventured further down that corridor, and indeed if Bruford and Moraz had ever worked together in a Yes context, in addition to their later collaboration (1983–1985) outside it.

As rhythm takes another turn

The *Relayer* album, eventually released in November 1974, was recorded in the late summer and autumn of that year at bassist Chris Squire's new studio at his home in Virginia Water, Surrey.

Operating from 'New Pipers' gave Yes a freedom and flexibility they had not enjoyed before. It also reduced costs, as it enabled them to use the studio as an instrument, not just as a way of realising pre-prepared music. Work began as a four-piece (Anderson, Howe, Squire and White) before Patrick Moraz eventually joined them, along with producer Eddy Offord. The resulting album has received a mixed to positive reception from critics writing both at the time and those revisiting it subsequently. It was also a relative commercial success (a reflection of the heyday of progressive rock), reaching number four on the UK Albums Chart, and rising to number five on the US Billboard top two hundred. *Relayer* has been re-mastered twice, in 2003 and in 2014, both with previously unreleased tracks. The 2014 edition, produced by Steven Wilson, includes new stereo and 5.1 surround sound mixes and additional tracks (alternatives, studio run-throughs, original stereo mixes, needle drops and an instrumental mix on Blu-ray).

No musical slouch himself, Patrick Moraz has said in a number of interviews over the years how impressed and even daunted he was watching Yes in action for the first time. To the Swiss musician their playing was fast and precise, and they seemed to have a ready connection with each other and with the music they were producing. It took the keyboard player a little time to tune into the band's musical dynamic, but he was a fast learner and soon found himself at the forefront of co-writing and co-production.

The project was well underway when he arrived, but the keyboard man was eager and capable of making important contributions to the process. Like *Close to the Edge*, the seventh Yes album ended up having one lengthy, major piece on it ('The Gates of Delirium' clocks in at 21' 55") and two shorter but nevertheless substantial songs, 'Sound Chaser' (9' 25") and 'To Be Over' (9' 06"). 'Gates' was already formed in the mind of Jon Anderson. He hammered it out to the band – badly, by his own account – on piano. Fortunately they got the key themes and ideas quickly and were able to take them forward. Moraz soon found himself integrated into the development of the piece, and he also played a key role with the opening section of 'Sound Chaser' and the closing fugal passages of 'To Be Over', among other contributions.

It is one of the many myths about Yes that the band has somehow been responsible for numerous 'concept albums', a belief that seems to have come about by transferring standard assumptions concerning prog rock onto any of the artists most centrally associated with the genre. In fact *Tales*, based on the Indian *shastras*, is the only thoroughgoing conceptual work, from beginning to end, that the band have produced. Certainly the track 'Close to the Edge' owes its origins in no small part to Jon Anderson's dalliance with Hermann Hesse. But the other two tracks were differently conceived. Similarly, *Relayer* is not a concept album *per se*, even if its lead piece, 'The Gates of Delirium', draws heavily upon ideas linked to Leo Tolstoy's epic historical novel, *War and Peace*. Like 'Ritual', the fourth side of *Tales*, it rehearses a long and painful life-struggle between the sources of good and light, and those of darkness and evil, sometimes clearly differentiated and sometimes less so.

The album cover by Roger Dean also reinforces the darker, questioning side of the band. A beautiful but threatening snake coils in the foreground. Warriors stalk the precipitous mountain ranges – close to the edge in a quite different way, indeed. There is an air of anticipation and menace, and more steel than colour. So too with the music, and with the poem that writer Donald Lehmkuhl crafted for the inner sleeve of the LP and for concert programmes, which concludes: "Truth conceals itself in error / History reveals its face / days of ecstasy and terror / invent the future that invents the race."

The Gates of Delirium

The opening bars of the main 21'56" work on *Relayer* (again, 'song' seems too paltry and restrictive a definition for the epic nature of what is to follow) illustrate that the musical language Yes are about to deploy has shifted yet again, beyond *Tales* and everything that went before it. This is a band projecting its musical ambitions forward apace. Jon Anderson says (in the *Yes-Years* documentary, 1991) that it was the first time he ever came to the band with a complete piece of music in his head, allowing them to develop it with him.

It falls into five continuous sections. An instrumental prelude (0.00–2:11), introducing some of key melodic and harmonic themes, a song section in which the central narrative ideas are set out (2:21–8:00), an instrumental 'battle sequence' (8:01–12:48) ending in an almost mocking carnival of triumph (12:49–16:08, and a gentle ballad ('Soon', 16:09–20:27) and coda (20:28–21:56) restoring a vision of peace after the churning tumult. Some 15 minutes of the piece is therefore instrumental, and it is the music that dictates the lyric pattern in the second section, rather than the other way round.

Synth, cymbals and a guitar sustain flutter atonally during the first few seconds of 'Gates', before Howe's Fender Telecaster establishes a first theme with a repeated call-and-response pattern, punctuated by Rhodes piano and ended each time with two dramatic notes from Squire's bass. An irregular metrical pattern and a second theme is developed between guitar and bass, with Moraz flitting across the keys and White staying with Squire's developing, primordial rhythmic statement. There is a suspended tonal pause lifted by a sequence of ascending pairs of notes from Howe as Anderson's vocals enter for the first time, announcing the conflict: "Stand and fight, we do consider / reminded of an inner pact between us."

Despite their occasional mannered archaisms, what follows are some of the best lyrics Yes co-founder Jon Anderson has ever forged, effectively exploring the psychology, ritual and dynamics of war in a warrior-driven culture. Patriotism, honour and the promise of glory make the battle seemingly inevitable, unavoidable and dutiful. The language suggests a historic setting, but the self-justifying sentiments are also disturbingly contemporary. The Vietnam War was still raging when 'Gates' was written, and although Yes are far from a political protest band, this is a piece of music that seeks to awaken us to the destruction we human beings are being lured into, and to promote the vision of another path in which (to quote Anderson introducing this song in 2001) "war is not needed".

There is a particularly poignant moment (5:45) when a voice of reason questions the rising tide of conflict: "Listen, should we fight for ever / Knowing as we do know / Fear destroys?" It is Squire's menacing bass, doubled by White's drums, that responds (6:19) with a typical *casas belli*: "Listen, your friends have been broken / They tell us of your poison / Now we know." The drive to war will not be thwarted. Here it is Howe's shrill guitar, set against an urgent rhythmic backdrop, that sets up the crashing, discordant finale, "pounding out the devil's sermon".

The instrumental 'battle sequence' proceeds on the basis of entirely new thematic material, involving guitar, keyboards, bass and drums. It builds and expands in two phases, the second involving a sudden change of tempo at 10:21. The tension continually increases. There is an insistent, staccato bass interruption at 10:46, to which Howe's Telecaster responds with peals of dissonance at 10:58. The staccato motif and second theme return, accompanied by terrifying shrieks and wails, an ever-rising and tightening momentum, a sudden increase in pace with Squire's stabbing bass (12:05), and finally the swirling keyboards and percussion that take us to the precipice of delirium (12:31). White's drums drag the beat back dramatically as we approach the very edge of insanity, where we are met by the onset of an orgiastic, triumphalist celebration of victory (12:49).

This is one of the most powerful moments in Yes's music over the years, as Moraz's wailing synths and White's thunderous drums drag Squire's bass into a series of swooping descents, while Howe weaves his slide guitar in and out of the revolving sequence until it exhausts and slows itself into a diminishing dynamic revolving around four concluding notes on bass. This extended instrumental section is as far as can be imagined from Bruford's "sunny, diatonic, A-major band" (*passim*). It also features some of the most adventurous and technically demanding work heard on any Yes album from Howe, Squire and White, joined by Moraz.

Time is once again suspended by floating synth sounds at 20:25, as we enter the gentle finale. "Soon, oh soon the light / Pass within and soothe this endless night," intones Anderson, against the backdrop of Howe's strummed acoustic guitar and Moraz's gentle keyboards. The tranquility and innocent beauty of the song sits in stark contrast to the organised, aggressive chaos that precedes it. 'Soon' has often been performed as a standalone song at Yes concerts, but for me this is unsatisfactory. Its point and purpose is lost when it is ripped from its larger context in 'The Gates of Delirium', risking a saccharine rendition shorn of emotional power. The band re-enters for a couple of minutes at the end of the ballad, upping the tempo and volume to draw the whole 22-minute piece to a firm resolution, but then departing on ascending waves of orchestral synth. It is a stunning piece of music, combining an avant-garde aesthetic with the power of rock, touches of jazz, shuddering dissonance, pleading melody and moments of real harmonic sophistication.

Sound Chaser

Patrick Moraz's crazed Rhodes piano heralds the next segment of the ambitious *Relayer* album, as the band dive headlong into the appropriately named 'Sound Chaser' (9' 25"). The opening was something the Swiss keyboard virtuoso crafted in "one or two takes" during his audition, he reckons. The style of the piece overall is certainly jazz-fusion, though it doesn't particularly emulate anything else in the field at the time, has strong rock (and some funk) components, and utilises left-field vocal harmonies. It is a *tour de force* performed at breakneck speed, featuring rapid-fire bass and some stunning work on drums from Alan White (for example 0:33-1:05). Moraz's keyboards project us into space before Howe's ferocious five-stage riff (1:04-1:13) prepares us for Jon Anderson's involved two-verse scene setter: "Faster moment spent spread tales of change within the sound / Counting form through rhythm / electric freedom." It's an evocation of the untamed vitality of being lost in music, but also held in the eyes of one you love.

At 2:06 the instrumental frenzy returns, catapulting all four musicians into Howe's landmark solo (3:00-4:13), backed by Moraz. The two were to argue over the right tone and balance of the keyboard accompaniment here, with the guitarist winning out but Moraz remaining less than satisfied with his space in the mix. The frenetic Telecaster solo was done in an 'as live' take. It is one of the guitarist's finest moment with Yes – full of grating sound and fury, but also delicacy and an almost Baroque, volume pedal and sustain twist at the end (4:14-5:31). It is truly a thing of beauty and refinement. Anderson returns with a single quiet reprise of the vocal strand ("As rhythm takes another turn / As is my want I only reach / To look in your eyes"). This is a prelude to yet more instrumental fireworks, taking the original Rhodes line and a brief bass/drum duel as their point of departure (6:11-6:27). Now a swinging new theme kicks in at 6:28, swaying, syncopating and switching tempo five times. Three-and-a-half primal "cha-cha-cha – cha-cha" chants interrupt the already punctuated flow, before Moraz bursts through with an attention-grabbing, monumental Moog break (7:45-8:35). It is piercing, fast and finished off with some judicious pitch bending. Howe and Squire fire off another flurry of notes in double-time, with Moraz improvising over the top, before the chanting returns (9:02) three times and the band performs its own three-point instrumental turn for their exit. Steve Howe (Morse 1996) sees the track as benefitting especially from the "indescribable mixture of Patrick's jazzy keyboards and my weird sort of flamenco electric [guitar]." It is certainly a curious brew, and it fair takes the breath away every time I hear it.

Just as *Relayer* borrowed its title from a lyric in 'The Revealing Science of God', so 'Sound Chaser' was named from a phrase in 'The Remembering' on *Tales From Topographic Oceans*. It was used as an opener in many concerts, most notably the famous shows at Boston Gardens in December 1974, Stoke and Queens Park Rangers in 1975 and Roosevelt Stadium, New Jersey, in 1976. The QPR gig was recorded (see discography), and there are unofficial recordings of the others. While the song is undoubtedly a fiery launchpad for any concert, it was often bedevilled by sound problems in that role. Interestingly, in his 2000 Star Licks Master Series video interview with the late Bob Birch (bass player with Elton John, Billy Joel and others), Chris Squire says that he sometimes used a riff from 'Sound Chaser' (8:39–8:44) as a warm-up exercise before going on stage.

To Be Over
After the violence of 'Gates' and the frenetic workout that is 'Sound Chaser', *Relayer* rests the listener in far softer waters with the elegiac, balmy, almost soothing 'To Be Over'. It originated in a melody and lyrical idea shared between Jon Anderson and Steve Howe, apparently elaborated by the guitarist after a boat ride on The Serpentine in Hyde Park, London. Talking to *Circus* magazine in February 1975, Howe described the track as "strong in content, but mellow in overall attitude," adding simply: "It's [essentially] about how you should look after yourself when things go wrong." The healing vibe is present from the outset, with guitar and keys laying out two gentle, contrapuntally entwined themes (0:16–1:18), highlighted by acoustic guitar, which recur in more elaborate form at the conclusion of the

piece. It is hauntingly beautiful.

Bass and drums pick up the thread at 1:47, as Jon Anderson and Chris Squire enter with the harmonised song component: "We go sailing down the calming streams / drifting endlessly by the bridge / To be over / We will see." It's a hazy, pastoral image, grounded by Squire's bass pinpricks and White's light drums, until Howe's steel guitar picks up the pace and projects us into an almost Caribbean bluesy jazz segment (3:05). The guitar solo at 3:45 is bright and resonant, opening into an orchestrally rich theme carried by the whole band (4:29). Guitar and synth, as throughout much of the album, are the focal point – while Chris Squire and Alan White work their magic in and with the lead lines. It is all exquisitely well formed.

The "Child like / Soul dreamer" song section that follows employs near-classical harmony. Moraz and Howe duet on a jazzy, Baroque theme (6:40) underpinned by Squire's harmonic bass. The final point of arrival is heralded by a moment of unabashed grandeur (7:15-7:31) before the song concludes with a fabulous synth/guitar counterpoint (7:32-9:05), further sketched out with bass and background vocals. Moraz wrote this section "exactly like a classical fugue", he says. He had scored an initial version the evening before rehearsing and recording, but amendments from others in the band caused him to spend more time recasting it in an overnight session. The result is well worth the effort. 'To Be Over' has not been played in concert by Yes since July 1975 in New Jersey, USA, despite numerous requests. But Steve Howe has used an acoustic guitar reduction of it for solo slots in 2003, 2009, 2010 and 2011. There is some hope that it might make a long overdue reappearance in 2018 or 2019.

Assessing a journey in sound
In a review published in December 1974, *Billboard* magazine called *Relayer* "another nearly flawless effort" by Yes. It noted

that Patrick Moraz "fits in perfectly" with the band. Sadly, the chemistry did not last beyond 1976, when Brian Lane and Chris Squire collaborated to get Rick Wakeman back for the *Going for the One* sessions in Switzerland and a subsequent commercially successful reunification with the band just when punk was alleged to be destroying prog. Those who were less complimentary about *Relayer* had the album rather too readily pigeon-holed as a follow-up to *Tales From Topographic Oceans*, even though the two projects, while both exploratory, are quite different in terms of style, content, texture and sound sources. However, along with side three of *Tales*, 'The Ancient', *Relayer* certainly stands out from the rest of the Yes catalogue as the most free-form and experimental work the group has ever produced.

Much of that is down to the battery of keyboards Moraz brought in to the studio, including Fender Rhodes 73 and 88 electric pianos, a D6 Clavinet, MiniMoogs and Mellotrons (of course) an ARP Pro, a Hammond C3 organ, an electric harpsichord and more. This was matched by Steve Howe's Sitar Coral, an EH 150 Steel, and a Fender Telecaster modified with a humbucker in the neck position and another pickup selector switch (fed through an amp at high volume). At the time of *Relayer*, he was also using a Dual Showman for main guitar and a Fender Quad Reverb for steel. It was these instruments, the clever arrangements and the close recording at New Pipers that gave the album such a distinctive sound, brought to life and clarified once more by Steven Wilson's 5.1 mix in 2014.

Chapter 7
Here We Can Be
(*Going for the One*)

Music gives colour to the air of the moment.

– Karl Lagerfeld

Almost three years after the appearance of *Relayer,* the world and music culture had moved on. In particular, the movement bearing the name 'punk rock' had emerged. Rooted in 1960s garage, it became a social and aural protest against the alleged elitism and gargantuan excesses of 1970s stadium rock and the rapid commercialisation of the 'music business'. That was until it became the latest consumer fad itself. At any rate, by the time Yes released *Going for the One* in July 1977, progressive rock was already being pronounced dead, or at least dubiously and possibly fatally malodorous.

It is ironic, then, that Yes – returning from a period in 1975 and 1976 in which the emphasis had been on solo projects to re-galvanise the band's creative mojo – were still selling out huge venues across the world in '77. Indeed, *Going for the One* reached number one in the UK Albums Chart for two weeks and peaked at number eight on the US Billboard top 200. This is illustrative of the fact that, contrary to the way much popular music history is written, punk and New Wave did not kill

Yes or prog. That was done more by its absorption into the radio-friendly blandishments of Adult- or Album-Oriented Rock. AOR was an assault on musical creativity by the FM and record company money barons. It was far more inimical to the free and rebellious spirit of punk than a few art-oriented musicians on the receding horizon of the 'progressive' scene. Sure, Lester Bangs hyperbolically traduced Emerson, Lake and Palmer (soon dubbed Cumbersome, Fake and Trauma) as 'war criminals' for carting their pantechnicons and theatrical stage antics around the globe. But most prog was not in this vein, even if its more commercially successful exponents were prone to self-parody from time-to-time, including Yes in a few of their mid-70s shows. "We were trying to put on Aida every night. It was killing us," Jon Anderson soberly observed on the other side of the mammoth *Tales From Topographic Oceans*, *Relayer* and solo album tours. The outcome was that, returning together and observing the changing music scene, something changed within Yes, too. The final result – not without its commercial element – was the departure of the more *avant garde* Patrick Moraz from the keyboard riser, and the return of Rick Wakeman, who had in the meantime become a glitzy showman of the kind that respectable punks despised, and perhaps not without reason.

Wakeman's return to Yes inevitably meant a retreat from the experimental and modernist horizons of *Tales* and *Relayer*, two albums with which he found little to no connection. There is a dispute about how much Moraz helped to shape *Going for the One* before he was replaced. He was certainly involved in early sessions in 1976, and he claims that material in his 'Time For a Change', released on the album *Out in the Sun* shortly before Yes's new opus appeared, is evidence of his input into the majestic and iconic 'Awaken'. There is more about this question at the end of the Chapter. What is beyond dispute is that *Going for the One* was a return to the less complicated sonorities of an earlier Yes, that of the *Fragile* era. It had five tracks rather than the three each on *Close to the Edge* and *Relayer,* and four across the double-album of *Tales.* It had denser instrumentation and harmony than the Yes of 1971, certainly. The production gave it a thick, cavernous quality at times, as if delivered in a cathedral or a dome. But much of the music itself, and for the most part the lyrical style, was simpler, clearer and closer to a mainstream rock vocabulary.

Visual and aesthetic clues

I remember well when I first unearthed *Going for the One* on a summer's day in central London. I had heard on the grapevine that Yes had been putting together new music, so I had been perusing record shops occasionally to see if anything had emerged. That's how things often were in pre-Internet age. I spent most of my time in the classical section of the shop in those days, but popped downstairs periodically to check the 'Y' category in rock, just in case. On Wednesday 27th July 1977, my luck was in, and my hands were soon clasping a pristine copy of the latest Yes release.

The first thing to notice, of course, was that in place of the Roger Dean fantasy art covers of the previous four albums, Storm Thorgerson and Aubrey Powell of Hipgnosis had created a photographic montage setting a skyscraper-defined urban landscape against the naked human form, intersected by lines of what looked like digital light. Inside, by contrast, was a picture of the band relaxing on the shores of Lake Geneva, near to the recording studio in the idyllic setting of Montreux, a municipality in the district of Riviera-Pays-d'Enhaut in the canton of Vaud in Switzerland – home also to the famous jazz festival where the band has performed.

There are, if you choose, multiple metaphors in all of this. First, the dominant images are notably earth-bound, rather than primarily ethereal. The same could be said about significant elements of the music on the album, and the artistic aspirations of the group at that time. But, equally, there is a sense of the smallness of humanity and the 'soft machine' s/he inhabits when compared to the sheer size of the physical universe, located in the shifting sands of time and space. In the middle of these depictions lie "the workings of man", to quote from the lyrics of 'Awaken', the album's 15-minute-plus highlight, which concerns the spiritual ascent and wanderings of humanity in history, culture and an emerging future.

Martin Popoff (*Time and A Word*, 2016) writes of the outside cover combining "slick, futuristic geometric urban angles with a man in his birthday suit, perhaps urgently propelling the band forward, while simultaneously embracing roots." That could be it, too. All this might seem to signify that while Yes had not lost their ambition and drive, there was a correspondingly greater concern to relate their music to the life-world of the audience. If *Tales* and *Relayer*, in particular, can be seen as works of art requiring the listener to adapt to their considerable demands, *Going for the One* attempts to bridge the gap between what people want and what they might receive, musically speaking. Many therefore identify this album as the transition (or alternatively, the descent) of the Yes from truly progressive music to stadium rock.

Going for the One

The massive change is nowhere more evident than in the eponymous opening track. 'Going for the One' (5' 30") is Yes delivering straight-ahead, albeit cleverly articulated and elliptical, rock'n'roll. From Steve Howe's count-in (contrasting with 'And You and I'), to the opening bluesy wail, to the steel guitar work that defines the song, past the wryly self-mocking lyrics ("Now the verses I've sang / Don't add much weight / To the story in my head / So I'm thinking I should go and write a punch line") and on to a stream-of-consciousness litany (3:25-4.48) - paralleling 'Siberian Khatru' in a lighter vein - this is Yes in a very different register. It is as if they were consciously trying to kick accusations of over-elaboration and pretentiousness into touch from the outset. As indeed they probably were. My first reaction, I confess, was one of horror. Only years later would I come to appreciate both the determination and the multilayered craft in this iconoclastic move.

Turn of the Century

For those left shocked by this musical kick-in-the-shins, a sense of balance was immediately restored by the beautiful, lyrical and expansive ballad, 'Turn of the Century' (7' 58"). Based around the Pygmalion myth, first re-introduced to public consciousness by George Bernard Shaw in 1913, this song is one of the most impressive illustrations of the sheer delicacy of Yes music, combined with its sonic and emotional power. Howe's sensitive acoustic guitar, Anderson's soaring lyrics, the harmony and balance introduced by Squire on bass and vocals, Wakeman's teaming keyboard runs and White's restrained percussion combine perfectly. The instrumental section (9:23–10.45) involving piano, steel guitar, bass and drums in layers of counterpoint, is one of my favourite moments in the band's extensive catalogue. It reaches a fabulous climax as we exit a more cerebrally complex zone and are met by a burst of sunlight and harmonic affirmation. Howe's fast, circular guitar motion and White's timpani theme are joyful and elevated, before we climb back down again to a quiet acoustic ending, full of reflective tenderness. It is an exquisite piece of music. How US critic Tony Ciarochi (*Fairbanks Daily News-Miner,* 6 August 1977) found it partly "monotonous", I really have no idea. Then again, it is genuinely possible for two people to hear something quite different from the same arrangement of notes, and the fact that Yes music can frequently divide hearers like this is, in a strange way, a testimony to its artistry and unpredictability.

Parallels

Chris Squire's 'Parallels' (5' 52") is next up, introduced by a few seconds of meditative tuned percussion before Rick Wakeman's church organ bursts in. It is a fairly routine song rendered almost overwhelmingly grand by epic instrumentation and orchestration. The organ was recorded 'down the line' from St Martin's Church in Vevey and synched in. It swings wonderfully with Squire's thunderous bass and Howe's searingly clean, swelling guitar lines, which surge and sing at 2:37 especially. The lyrics reflect the writer's humanistic and optimistic view of human capacity fired by the ambition and directionality of passion realised. I can still hear broadcaster Derek Jewell intoning the final stanza on BBC Radio 3's 'Sounds Interesting' programme: "No hesitation when we're all about / To build a shining tower / No explanations need to work it out / You know we've got the power." It is statement of audacious conviction that conveys and matches the music perfectly. Wakeman's organ solo (3:28-3.58) is another standout moment, often replaced by Moog in concert. Overall, this is a song to lift the soul, and one which came from the sessions for Chris Squire's superb solo album, *Fish Out of Water*. The unlikely church organ and drums combination was, incidentally, one that jazz musicians Asif Sirkis and Steve Lodder would reprise on their superb *Inner Noise* debut in 2003.

Wonderous Stories
At 3' 38", the floating, climbing, tantalisingly textured 'Wonderous Stories' (*sic*) is almost a palate cleanser before the final feast on *Going for the One*. A surprise hit as a single for Yes, it has been described by Jon Anderson as a "dream sequence" in which the hearer is transported to and from a higher plane of consciousness. Wakeman's tumbling waterfalls of harpsichord, Howe's strummed acoustic, Squire's tuneful bass and White's gentle counter-rhythms combine to carry the lyrics forward in waves. It is a gorgeous miniature illustrating the grace and elegance that Yes could summon so readily at this time. Yet it is also entirely accessible.

Awaken

From rocky glaciers to faraway ranges and dreamy foothills, *Going for the One* takes us on a musical and emotional journey of many layers and contrasts. The best, however, is still to come. Against some who see it merely as an overblown cycle of fifths, I would rate 'Awaken' as one of the band's finest achievements – signalling Yes at the height of their powers, along with the three full albums that precede this one. The studio version lasts 15' 37". In concert it usually extends to 18 or 19 minutes. The performance at the Montreux Festival (2003), appropriately enough, is one of the best-filmed live recordings of the piece. Also well worth listening to are Jon Anderson's non-Yes orchestral rendition with Icelandic musicians Todmobile (2013) and the extended 22-minute version produced by Anderson Rabin Wakeman (ARW) in 2016–17.

'Awaken' is essentially a song cycle. Introduced by Wakeman's cascading piano (0:00–00:35), it is book-ended by two dreamy sequences where the opening and closing lyrical stanzas, developed slightly at the end, are suspended in one of those synth-led unfixed tonal spaces, accompanied by Sho-Bud pedal steel, where time feels as if you are floating in space (00:36–1:33): "High vibration go on / To the sun, oh let my heart dreaming / Past all mortal as we / Where can I be?"

The transition from questioning lyrics to a driving instrumental flourish is marked by a single bass note (1:27), detailed vocal harmonising ("Here we can be") and Howe's swooping guitar. In the 'Gentle-Mass-Touching' sequence he is using a Mapleglo Rickenbacker 360 12-string, while Squire's bass growls underneath (1:55–2:00) and White's drums emphasise the accents of the other instruments. Anderson enters with the propelling, accompanied chant ("strong dreams reign here"). At 2:50 Howe's guitar unfolds a fast, ascending set of figurations, joined by

Wakeman's synth (3:42). There is a brief recapitulation (3:57–4:20), before the instruments combine to puncture the flow with a descending motif finally lifted by Moog into the next development. There is an abrupt change of tempo (5:10) as Wakeman's church organ herald's the "Workings of man / Set to ply out historical life" vocal section. Here the old, grand Yes is in full flow and lyrical flourish. You either love it or hate it. After Squire's staccato bass notes a burst of organ brimming with magnificence (5:45–5:55) leads us into what appears to be a climax ("All is left for you now", 6:03) but which flowers colorfully and then pulls back shyly (6:28) almost as quickly as it appeared.

The middle section of 'Awaken' drifts in on synth, harp and crotales (6.35) before Wakeman's reedy, flute-like church organ comes into focus, exchanging and extending phrases until a more full-throated theme appears (7:36). Finally the organ is joined and intertwined with synth (8:34), supplemented by the lightest percussive touches. It reaches into a swelling and then diminishing motion until guitar and harp reappear. This magically unreal atmosphere is finally transfigured by an almost Baroque guitar figure (9:53–10:15) on Howe's Fender Telecaster. Synth and organ rejoin the fray. There is another partial, exultant climax (10:28–10:37), until Anderson's vocal returns with a fresh refrain ("Master of images / Songs cast a light on you").

This section, which is joined by the church organ, is Yes music at its most unashamedly glorious, sonorous, layered and powerful. It is enhanced with abstract choral passages performed by the Richard Williams Singers, with musical arrangements by Wakeman, and the Ars Laeta of Lausanne, recorded at the Église des Planches in Montreux. At this point, the listener is simply swept away ("Be honest with yourself / There's no doubt, no doubt…"). Howe makes his guitar fly and sing (11:25), and Squire's bass positively surges (11:44). The instruments combine towards the vocal summit (11:57) as Anderson reaches the peak: "And as we look forever closer / Shall we now bid... / Farewell, farewell." Just when it feels as if the music can go no higher, Wakeman returns with an absolutely glorious church organ passage. It is possibly the most impressively direct creation of his time with Yes, soaking up every ounce of his training and sensibility into one mountaintop musical *dénouement*.

I have seen this, and Howe's guitar interjections, referred to as 'solos'. That misses the point entirely. These are individual components of a seamless musical garment in which the players weave in and out of the light and shade, spurred on or restrained by the changing dynamics, to drive home the sublime whole. Then, just as swiftly as we are taken to the highest point, we are brought down into the opening dream-like song. But this time, as T. S. Eliot says, we return to where we started and know the place for the first time. All the musical and lyrical preceding grandeur in response to the opening question ("Where can I be?") has subsided, and what we are left with is a moment that is both intensely personal and disarmingly simple. There is, in the end, Love. "Like the time I ran away / and turned around / and you were standing close to me." Chris Squire grounds the recapitulation and conclusion with a few choice, beautifully placed bass notes that sit on the edge of the tempo (as suggested by Alan White), before Steve Howe winds things up with an unpredictably light, almost insouciant, acoustic guitar wiggle.

'Awaken' is a quite extraordinary piece of music. It is one of Rick Wakeman's finest moments with the band, and an occasion of unsurpassed unity in what many still regard (notwithstanding the immense contributions of Bill Bruford, and others) as the 'classic' Yes line-up. Jon Anderson has often said that, for him, 'Awaken' is all he could hope for in a piece of music, and a true summation of what Yes at its apex is all about. The song has its critics and agnostics, of course. For some it is too grand, too elaborate, too *everything*. But in my experience it is a track that can soon determine whether a listener is going to discover fully the humming core of Yes music, or feel finally undecided by it. Incidentally, an early version of what became the song's introduction was first performed live by Moraz (thereby establishing his compositional title, perhaps) during the band's final concert on the *Relayer* tour, in Jersey City, USA, in July 1975.*

Going where next?
The *Going for the One* album was first reissued on CD across Europe in 1988. A digitally re-mastered version then followed in 1994. In 2003, Rhino and Elektra Records released a new digitally re-mastered CD with seven bonus tracks. These feature 'Vevey (Revisited)', which could justifiably (and not necessarily unkindly) be called 'noodling' on organ and harp, out of which the middle section of 'Awaken' was to emerge. A particular gem is 'Montreux's Theme'. It is led by a finely understated piece of bass composition and playing from Chris Squire, embellished and complemented by Steve Howe and Alan White. Moraz's keys can be heard faintly in the background. This is perhaps my favourite 'off the wall' little Yes vignette, and, along with much more of Squire's work, is rendered beautifully in a bass cover by the estimable Miguel Falcão, which can be found through his YouTube page online.

Other additional tracks include the studio version of Squire's take on John Newton's 'Amazing Grace' (which was played live regularly on the *90125* and *Union* tours, and is featured on *9012Live*), plus the fascinating 'Eastern Number' (12' 19") a proto-version of 'Awaken' that also appears to include Patrick Moraz on Novotron. It offers a further, interesting glimpse into the building blocks and byways of a classic song. Finally, 2013 saw two re-mastered 'audiophile' versions put out, one by Audio Fidelity for the Super Audio CD format and the other by

---

* For far more detail on this piece, see John R. Palmer's 'Yes, Awaken, and the progressive rock style' (*Popular Music*, May 2001) and Gary Hampson's 'Awaken: The transformative lyrics and music of the progressive rock group Yes' (independent.academia.edu, accessed 4 January 2018).

Friday Music releasing a 180-gram LP using the original tapes. For many Yes aficionados, *Going for the One* marks the end of a 'core sequence' in the band's output, from 1971 to 1977. Others mark the end of a 'classic' period at *Relayer*. Certainly, the album can be seen as some kind of watermark, and it posed the question of where the band might possibly go next, musically and artistically.

Chapter 8
Forward Out
This Feeling
(1978–1991)

Ten true summers long
We go round and round and round and round
Until we pick it up again

– Yes, 'Future Times/Rejoice'

So far we have proceeded at a considered, extended pace, rather like much of the defining music of Yes in the first nine years of the band's creative existence. Now we will begin to gather speed and sharpness, as the band career into the '80s and '90s, a period marked by a couple of highs and a number of lows.

Tormato
By the time Yes reassembled in Paris in 1979, failing to come up with any workable formula, the fissions in the band had become clear, and there was little that bringing in producer Roy Thomas Baker could do to repair them. But listening to and looking at *Tormato* (the chaotic cover image and title tells its own story), it is clear that the seeds of disruption can be found at the heart of this 1978 album. On the misshapen 'Arriving UFO' and in the

man-child fantasy of 'Circus of Heaven' (which oddly derives in part from a Ray Bradbury novel, apparently), Jon Anderson's tendency towards the bizarre or twee can be said to have compromised the common good. The orchestral pop of 'Onward' and the frantic New Wave-lite of 'Release, Release' – almost a manifesto for a quite different kind of Yes – added to the peculiarity of the overall mix.

Yet the creative, propulsive spirit of the band seemed very much alive in 'Future Times / Rejoice', on Chris Squire's bass-driven 'On the Silent Wings of Freedom' and in the instrumental sections of 'Don't Kill the Whale' (the band's first out-and-out attempt at a protest song, and a single that was actually ahead of the populist environmental curve at the time). 'Madrigal', meanwhile, was what it proclaimed itself to be: a delicate combination of harpsichord, acoustic guitar and angular vocal lines.

Listening back, what strikes me about *Tormato*, given its uncertain studio genesis, its mixed (more-often-than-not unfavourable) critical reception, and its uneven musical flavours, is how strongly some of it still comes across today. There was and is huge potential stored up in these curious collections of notes, and between the tantalising vinyl grooves. But, somehow, it could not be properly realised at this juncture in the group's often-tortuous history. What a singular composer has to overcome is inner fractures and tensions in the process of developing music that transcends individual fragility. But for a group of writers and performers the challenge is multiplied. When things are going well the synergy can be magical. On other occasions, it feels (and sounds) like a traffic jam. That, it seems to me, is *Tormato*. There were too many ideas and musicians trying to crowd each other out.

Even so, the standout tracks among the eight contenders are worthy successors to *Going for the One*. Alongside the aforementioned 'Madrigal' (shades of Howe with Moraz on 'Beginnings' in 1975, incidentally) 'Future Times / Rejoice' (6' 44') fuses two distinct but related song ideas. It has a driving pulse, carried by a mêlée of guitar, synth, bass and drums. It is punctuated by another brief 'suspended' section, and finally leaves us in mid-space. The production on *Tormato* has been roundly criticised, backed by the discovery that its tone was accidentally suppressed by Dolby. That said, and not uncontroversially, I actually enjoy Rick Wakeman's Birotron sound. This is a keyboard instrument using 8-track cartridge tapes to play sounds whenever a key is depressed. It is a similar concept to the Chamberlin and the Mellotron, and is a forerunner of digital sampling. It was used particularly for strings, choirs, brass and flutes. These were sounds not easily reproduced on synths at the time.

The instrument makes another telling entry on 'Arriving UFO', which has a couple of really lively and unusual instrumental passages, despite its lyrical quirkiness. The most compelling song of all on *Tormato,* however, is surely Chris Squire's underrated 'On the Silent Wings of Freedom' (7' 47"). Stretching Anderson's voice just a little too far at times, it is a remarkable bass workout with a strong developing theme, the now almost obligatory quiet and contained passage, and a ludicrously fast keyboard wig-out at the end. Glorious stuff. Nevertheless, this and the pretty 'Onward' (featuring arrangements by the late Andrew Pryce Jackman, and used to pay tribute to Chris Squire in 2015 and 2016 at the beginning of concerts) wasn't enough to rescue the album from an uncertain, partial musical space – even if the accompanying tours in 1978 and 1979 were a triumph.

It was clear that the '70s version of Yes could go no further. Indeed the band as a whole seemed to have reached a terminus. But, as has happened so often in Yes history, an unexpected twist opened up a new musical avenue. With Anderson and Wakeman bailing on the Paris sessions, a tour had been booked and an album was needed. So it was that the happenstance of postmodern pop pioneers Trevor Horn and Geoff Downes (aka The Buggles, replete with their hit 'Video Killed the Radio Star' and later *Adventures in Modern Recording*) were working in an adjoining studio. This eventually led to one of the most unexpected alliances in progressive rock. Horn, with a contorted high tenor range and dystopian lyrical ideas took the band's front microphone, while Downes moved the Yes keyboard sound in a much more textured, modern direction. The result was a surprisingly successful new album. *Drama* took the idea of prog and dragged it through a punchy, New Wave hedge backwards. At the time it was received with suspicion by many Yes fans and surprise by many critics. Horn's voice could not sustain regular concert performances, but it was curiously appealing on record. Downes brought a whole new sensibility to the deep structure of the Yes sound, and was also willing *not* to play where that was the better choice, unlike the sometimes musically incontinent Wakeman.

Drama

The *Drama* album (1980) saved Yes and projected the band into a very different future. In many respects it bridges the 1970s and the 1980s. Revived in full only recently, it has acquired pretty much the status of a Yes classic, being championed by, among others, producer/musician Steven Wilson and new bassist Billy Sherwood, who both have it as a favourite Yes album alongside *Tales From Topographic Oceans*. That might seem an odd combination, but strangely it works, and will find a fresh audience again during the band's 2018 fiftieth anniversary concerts.

Featuring a stormy, image laden cover from Roger Dean, *Drama* opens with a foreboding slice of melodrama, 'Machine Messiah', which explores how the human spirit can survive or flourish in the shadow of manipulated big technology. The music is almost (to adapt a phrase once used for King Crimson's iconic *Red*) 'heavy metal for intellectuals', though with plenty of light, shade and a certain quirky 'Yesness' in the – albeit darker

– lyrical effusions. There is some fierce drumming from White, demanding parts for Squire on bass, Howe's questing Gibson Les Paul, and the inclusion from Downes of an arpeggiated segment from the fifth movement of Charles-Marie Widor's Organ Symphony Number 5. The new, slick Yes might have had "an oil change", as publicist Dan Hedges once cutely put it, but they were still capable of their old musical tricks.

Following on from the 10' 27" opener (a 'normal' length of song for Yes) came an unusual miniature. 'Man in a White Car' is a sardonic, monotonic commentary on Gary Numan's automobile flights of fantasy, recorded by Downes in an afternoon on a Fairlight CMI. Horn's vocals and a vocoder were then mixed in. The piece has a tiny Baroque ornamentation at the end, which was sadly excised from live performances in 2016. It is a cute little vignette.

Meanwhile, 'Does It Really Happen' (6' 34"), featuring a muscular, time-dropped bass riff, came from the Paris sessions. In many way it prefigures '90s Yes, abandoning Andersonian whimsy for something much more sinewy, and with an out-of-silence trumpet voluntary style synth payoff at the end.

'Into the Lens' is another singularly good piece of music, built around a lyrical theme that ends up paralleling Christopher Isherwood's famous quote in his *Goodbye to Berlin* Weimar novel (1939): "I am a camera with its shutter open, quite passive, recording, not thinking." Here Yes use stop and start motifs to take the musical and lyrical narrative forward in stages. The vocoder also makes another appearance. The original material was from Horn and Downes, developed by Squire and the others.

'Run Through the Light', however, was a song that originally featured Jon Anderson, but on *Drama* acquired some interesting instrumental variations. Horn, a capable bassist, took that role. Squire played the piano part. Howe added some melancholic, pleading parts on his Les Paul and Martin Mandolin, while Downes sweeps the whole thing along with rounded synth and White nails it to the floor on and just off the beat.

The final offering on Drama was the addictive, propulsive 'Tempus Fugit', featuring Howe's ska-inflected Fender Stratocaster lines, and especially Squire's Elektra bass with the distinctive flanger module built into the body. Lionel Gibaudan and Miguel Falcão have produced a good transcription of the trebly bass part (YouTube), which is the foundation of the whole song – revived again in concert in 2009/10 and again in 2016/17. There were attempts to persuade Jon Anderson to tackle this piece during his later reappearances in Yes, but they never worked out. Trevor Horn joined Jon Davison on stage for 'Tempus Fugit' with the band at their Oxford and London dates in 2016. Overall *Drama* was well received (perhaps a little more so outside the band's immediate circle) and has endured very well indeed. Rick Wakeman dismissed it early on, but then came around to seeing how pivotal it was in moving Yes forward.

The band broke up after the *Drama* tour, with Chris Squire and Alan White keeping the rhythm section flame alive with the orchestrally accompanied Christmas-themed single, 'Run With the Fox', and an instrumental B-side version) in 1981. Howe and Downes formed Asia, while Squire and White continued to write together, eventually forming Cinema in 1982 with virtuoso South African guitarist and singer/songwriter Trevor Rabin. With Anderson being brought back in, this led to the recovery of Yes and the development of the next album from the band, which turned out to be its eight-million strong worldwide best seller.

90125

It was quite by accident that I first heard *90125* (released in November 1983) in early 1984, having thought that Yes had disappeared off the scene following *Drama*. It was another shock. The track in question, flitting across my ears from a neighbour's radio, was 'Leave It'. There was something reminiscently Yes-like about those multilayered vocal harmonies and the acapella fed through a Synclavia. Jon Anderson's alto tenor voice clinched the deal. Yet, simultaneously, it sounded nothing like received music from the band. The album has, indeed, little to do with the 1971–1977 Yes era, other than the vocal inflexions, Squire's trademark bass and the return of organist Tony Kaye alongside a beefed up Alan White on drums. In every other respect, not least Rabin's scalar, blues-based guitar and a 'stadium sound', it is a different band. By this stage, Trevor Horn had moved away from the microphone and into the producer's chair. *90125* had a cutting edge '80s sound, with plenty of finesse in the mix for those looking for such touches.

'Owner of a Lonely Heart' echoed back to the Beatles' *Sergeant Pepper* with its title. It was covered ironically by Frank Zappa, featured a blistering James Brown sample from the horn section of 'Kool is Back' by Funk, Inc., and stormed the charts on both sides of the Atlantic and beyond. It took Yes into a new dimension – one in which its past glories were in danger of being eclipsed. Geoff Downes told Tim Morse in 1994 that Rabin and Horn's mini-masterpiece was a mixed blessing for the band, giving it resources but pulling it in a problematic direction. It is undeniably a really well-crafted song and is often expanded instrumentally in concert – including a gloriously bombastic instrumental prelude from the front of 'Make It Easy' (*YesYears*). Rabin's solo utilises a harmoniser set a perfect fifth apart plus one octave. Bill Bruford once said he preferred the song's straightforward honesty to a mere regurgitation of a past prog style. In that respect it has perhaps surprising allies. 'Owner' does not give anything like a good indication of Yes in-depth, of course. But there are other tracks on *90125*, a title adapted from the label number, that work slightly better in that respect. 'Hearts' (7' 34"), though a little cloying, is probably the most traditionally Yes-like song on the album, with Anderson's sweet lyrics and harmonies sounding like very early Yes updated. It works well live. In between, as a prelude to the vocally dense 'Leave It', we have the 1984 Grammy-winning 2' 09" metallic, sheeny instrumental 'Cinema', recorded live at AIR Studios. It is in fact the beginning of an unreleased and probably uncompleted 20-minute piece called 'Time'. As well as being used as an opener on the 1984/5 tour, it has also been reprised several times more recently and was readapted by Anderson Rabin Wakeman in 2016/17.

Not without its internal rhythmic tricks, 'Hold On' (5' 15") follows 'Owner', addressing the brooding politics of the world with a strong plea not to succumb. Its huge backbeat and broad stadium sound was a new departure for the band, picked up again in 1994's *Talk*. 'It Can Happen' (5' 39"), by contrast, is dainty and ornamented by a sitar guitar. Composed at the piano by Chris Squire, Trevor Rabin crafted the guitar part to fit it. At 3'13 it samples lines from acting legend Laurence Olivier, taken from Oscar Wilde's *The Importance of Being Earnest*. 'Changes' (6' 16") is one song on the album for which Steve Howe has shown some enthusiasm. It opens with compound meter and alternating bars of 7/4 and 10/4 before Rabin's wailing climax bridges into a relatively conventional song.

By contrast, 'Our Song' (4' 16") has a fanfare beginning, an irregular beat and counterpoint components. It works very well indeed, reminding us that, "Music is a shout of foregone conclusions / As long as music plays its part / good, good part."

Last but not least we have the harsh, grinding 'City of Love' (4' 48"), pressing the dystopian button hard lyrically and using shards of metallic guitar crunch to make its impact into what in concert can be a three-minute instrumental workout. Overall, then, *90125* is a fine album with far more interest and built-in subtlety than much pop-prog. But it's hard to see it as a landmark for Yes music *per se*, other than commercially.

Big Generator

After a monumental world tour, Yes regrouped, but found it difficult to get material together, find a place to record and resolve a tension between the two mighty Trevor's, Horn (on his way to becoming a world famous producer) and Rabin (whose sights would increasingly be set on Hollywood film scoring). Missing several industry beats along the way, *Big Generator*, when it finally appeared in 1987, sounded incredibly shiny and blended together elements of the sound and approach that had made *90125* so viable, while returning to some of the subtleties of an earlier Yes in a new setting. The swinging, diving opener, 'Rhythm of Love' (4' 47"), proceeds from an intimately scored string arrangement. It features Brazilian star Paulinho Da Costa on additional percussion and has been rearranged several times live to include new keyboard parts. The title track (4' 33"), meanwhile, is almost 'Machine Messiah' from *Drama*, part two. It lurches and leans on the beat, utilising as its thumping theme a meaty riff from Squire's Tobias five-string guitar. One of the heaviest moments in Yes music, it reflects once again on the human/technology relationship for good or ill.

With 'Shoot High, Aim Low' (7' 01") we enter the territory of the three most substantial songs on *Big Generator*. Taking its world-beyond-war lyric from the CIA-fuelled conflict in Nicaragua in the mid 1980s, the song features an alternating counterpoint vocal, 'dreamtime' versus 'real time'. Rabin's guitar solo, with its Spanish shimmer, was extended in concert, as can be heard on the *Word is Live* (2005) recording. It features natural reverb from the castle where it was recorded, in Carimate, Italy. "On stage, 'Shoot High, Aim Low' was magical," Jon Anderson recalled to *Something Else* magazine in 2014. "I was pushing the band back to doing Yes music, basically." It has "poise and expansiveness", reckons commentator Kevin Mulryne.

A quite different mood is projected by 'Almost Like Love' (4′ 58″), which oddly is one of my favourites on the album, featuring a stream of consciousness Anderson rap, a gorgeous central motif, and descending horn section played by Nick Lane (trombone), James Zavala and Greg Smith (sax), and Lee Thornburg (trumpets). It also has a screaming guitar riff. It is not to everyone's taste, but I think it adds something quite special. "Saint or sinner / Makes no difference in who you believe / In a world of superstition / Caught in a total nuclear greed," declares the vocalist.

'Love Will Find a Way' is one of what could be regarded as two missteps on *Big Generator*. An undeniably lush, beautifully melodious song with a crafted string arrangement by Rabin again, it was originally slated for a Stevie Nicks (Fleetwood Mac) record. Then drummer Alan White pulled it back for the new Yes album. Another attempt by ATCO Records to curate a 'hit', it is of undeniable quality in its own right, but stands out as odd in a Yes context. The other song that struggles to work for the whole is Jon Anderson's 'Holy Lamb', which starts in a register too low for him to be comfortable with, builds to a suitable climax, but somehow lacks the kind of arrangement that could deliver it into the stratosphere to which it aspires.

The remaining two tracks offer something interesting and different. 'Final Eyes' (6′ 25″) takes its title from a verbal pun. It has a slightly melancholy feel instrumentally, and is structured to accommodate several changes of mood. Trevor Rabin, who crafted it, was not entirely happy with the structure in the end. For me the great prize of the album, however, is 'I'm Running'. It really is a magnificent piece of music, taking Yes back to the scope and ambition of the 1970s, though still with a distinctive '80s feel. The opening Latin/Caribbean style riff on Squire's five-string bass sets the scene. The winding melody and harmony builds beautifully throughout the song, with layer upon layer being added towards an almost *bel canto,* polyphonic choral climax. It can be accused of being overdone, and was one of a number of complex features that made this piece difficult to realise effectively in concert. It has therefore only been performed on four occasions, along with 'Final Eyes'. The song itself is a plea to run away from human-made terror and towards the conscious simplicity of life and love. Its immediate context is the threat to human flourishing of nuclear testing, a theme Anderson would return to in the song 'Birthright' (see below): "A simple peace / Just can't be found / Waste another day / Blasting all their lives away / I've heard the thunder / Underground / Tunneling away / At the very soul of man." The vocal treatments are what make or break 'I'm Running'. For me, it is a highlight of the so-called 'Yes West' (Californian-centred) years.

Anderson Bruford Wakeman Howe

After *Big Generator,* Anderson decided that Yes was in danger of straying too far from the original Yes ideal, and re-united with the other side of the band – guitarist Steve Howe, drummer Bill Bruford (now looking for contexts to explore a tonally based Simmons electric kit) and keyboardist Rick Wakeman. Bringing his erstwhile musical colleagues together for what was ostensibly assistance on a solo album, the singer combined with manager Brian Lane in the impresario role, creating a band that sounded peculiarly like a law firm – Anderson, Bruford, Wakeman, Howe. They duly completed an original, eponymously titled album in the holiday setting of Montserrat (June 1989), and then headed out for a very successful and lucrative *ABWH* tour. The resulting 'Evening of Yes Music Plus' caused some legal friction between the two sides of the Yes fold, ultimately resolved in the commercially driven decision to form an eight-piece and put two sets of recording efforts together in the *Union* album and tour (1991/2), explored in the next Chapter. That was something Anderson's colleagues did not set out to transition to. Indeed, Bruford and Howe, in particular, were keen to avoid the Yes entanglement with *ABWH* as far as possible, and to set about the task of producing new music with former colleagues who had gone off to have different experiences, rather than to try to reinvent Yes.

Bruford's Simmons percussion, in particular, helps create a different aural texture to *Anderson Bruford Wakeman Howe*. The intricacy, melody, harmony and rhythmic trickery are still there, but with a fresh and sometimes summery feel. On the pragmatically entitled 'Themes' (5' 58"), which sets out their instrumental stall, Anderson also pronounces on the business of music, which he has at once swum with and resented at different stages in his career: "Be gone you ever piercing / Power Play machine / Cutting our musical solidarity." With its multi-part format, mostly required for assigning publishing rights, the *ABWH* project was certainly evoking the Yes aura by default, and by the time it took to the stage, with supplementary musicians and virtuosos Tony Levin / Jeff Berlin taking 'the Squire role', this was firmly established in the minds of audiences, as Lane knew perfectly well it would be.

The second track of nine, 'Fist of Fire' (3' 27") focuses around a gothic theme and a burst of dense, synth-heavy keyboard fireworks from Wakeman. The 10' 18" 'Brother of Mine' suite combines modern song (with a writing contribution from Geoff Downes) and light instrumental textures for a piece that is both accessible and elaborate. 'Birthright' (6' 02", aided by another Howe collaborator, Max Bacon) picks up the nuclear testing issue in the context of the appalling experience of indigenous people at Maralinga, South Australia, between 1956 and 1963. It employs Bruford's electric kit to create a brooding atmosphere with hints of Aboriginal culture. It is perhaps the most original and interesting track on the album. Two ballads, 'The Meeting' (4' 21") and 'Let's Pretend' (2' 56", co-written by Vangelis, with whom Anderson had established a famous collaboration) provide a much lighter aspect to the album. They also cemented a specific partnership between Anderson and Wakeman that was to blossom further decades later and lead to albums such as *The Living Tree* (2010).

There is a more restrained acoustic version of the vocally-dominated 'Quartet' (9' 22", with Ben Dowling, referencing Yes classics such as 'Roundabout' and 'Long Distance Runaround'), which in my view works better than the sickly sweet album one. 'Teakbois' (7' 39"), meanwhile, is a gauche, calypso style tune that should have best been left on the cutting floor. 'Order of the Universe' (9' 02") points towards the old grandeur of Yes in a more rocky context, and is a highlight – though the central harmonies on the chorus were underwhelming live and really needed presets of the kind the west-coast band were understandably to use for vocally dense numbers like 'Leave It' and 'Rhythm of Love'.

Overall, *Anderson Bruford Wakeman Howe* was a mixed affair, though not without highlights and portents of the future. Bruford had nothing to do with the composition side, using this project (like the ill-fated *Union*) to enjoy a musical vacation with friends and to bank financial resources for his number one priority, jazz – and especially his high-end ensemble, Earthworks. Wakeman made contributions to 'Fist of Fire' and 'The Meeting'. But most of the heavy lifting was done by Anderson, Howe and allies, with Roger Dean providing a colourful, evocative cover featuring 'Blue Desert' on the front and 'Red Desert' on the back. A re-mastered limited edition version of the album appeared in March 2011, featuring live bonus material and an additional track, 'Vultures in the City' (5' 56"), which is a light, fairly breezy affair, albeit with weightier lyrical concerns. The next twist in the *ABWH* plot was, of course, to take everyone by surprise. And it is hard not to be struck by the five enormous leaps in contrary directions embodied in the five albums we have just considered.

Chapter 9
Speaking New Languages
(1991–1997)

> Music isn't just a pleasure, a transient satisfaction. It's a need, a deep hunger; and when the music is right, it's joy. Love. A foretaste of heaven.
>
> – Orson Scott Card

Sometimes Yes in the 1980s is spoken of as if it was one thing. But the four studio albums produced over that span were all, in their own ways, quite distinct. The complexity, experimentation, scale and musical elaboration of the 1972–1974 period had gone, for sure. But in its place came the taut 'new wave prog' of *Drama*, the prog-pop of *90125*, the neo-progressive elements of *Big Generator*, and the technologically finessed retro-prog of *Anderson Bruford Wakeman Howe*. Indeed it was the fusing of all these elements and more, driven by heavy commercial demands, that was eventually to produce the unwieldy package that is the *Union* album, released on 31 April 1991.

This hour-long collection of 14 tracks, emerging from the attempted fusion of *ABWH* and the west-coast US band, amounted to an uncomfortable 'Yes smorgasbord', which pretty much all the participants regret and resent. It gave talented producer Jonathan Elias an almighty studio headache and relied on an army of session players to attempt to recue the discontented members of both groups from artistic disaster. However, from the point of view of assessing the music itself, it is important to step back from the recriminations that marked this expensive, artificially engineered project and listen again. For me, that means revisiting the reactions I had well before I knew anything about the labyrinthine shenanigans involved.

Union

The first song, 'I Would Have Waited Forever' (6'32"), sets the pattern for what would otherwise have been a second *ABWH* album, albeit processed through the compositional and production predilections of Jonathan Elias. The texture is dense, with vigorous melody and layered harmony supplemented by crunchy guitar (Jimmy Haun plays a key role) and an almost industrial drum sound. The opening vocals have an American twang to them and the structure is interestingly complex. As Brian Wurzel, who holds a Licentiate of the Royal Academy of Music, wrote at the time for *Yes Music Circle* (June 1991):

> The track comprises eight contrasting musical ideas, four of them partly or entirely vocal. Altogether, these are presented sixteen times in four groups of decreasing length. Each group begins with a title refrain and ends with a different *non*-vocal idea of *increasing* length ... There is no classical form in anything like this, but only someone with classical experience could have created it.

That last comment applies to quite a bit of Yes's more elaborate music. Steve Howe employed a guitar riff from 'Sensitive Chaos' from his solo album *Turbulence* (1991) as a lengthy coda here. Elias argues (Chamber, 2002) that the track represents the best of "both early and late Yes styles."

The second song, 'Shock to the System' (5' 09"), is rather more straightforward and based on a strong 7-7-7-4-4 note riff. There is plenty of playing alongside the focal lyrics and a pleasing, quiet interlude. This tilt at power politics is followed by Howe's elegant, angled and stylistically mixed Spanish acoustic solo, 'Masquerade' (2' 17"), recorded at his home studio using a two-channel Revox deck. Next up is the first Yes west-coast contribution, the radio friendly but extended 'Lift Me Up' (6' 30"), which is prefaced by a repeated, chunky 2-4-2-4 rhythm. Trevor Rabin was not happy with the mix, but he certainly knew how to write a hook. This song could easily have appeared on the *90125* album, though Trevor Horn would undoubtedly have produced it differently.

'Without Hope (You Cannot Start the Day)' is another reasonably effective post-*ABWH* piece (5' 18"), originated by Elias and featuring the direct piano parts that he used to replace what Wakeman had supplied, "which sounded like a Rachmaninoff piano concerto" (Morse, 1996). It is an angularly styled song with some solid rhythmic work and instrumentation, but also sounds a little bit like 'Yes by numbers' at times. The same cannot be said for the cod-reggae pop song, 'Saving My Heart' (4' 41"), which, as Rabin agrees, simply should not have made the cut.

'Miracle of Life', by contrast, is one of the best pieces on *Union*. It is the longest track at 7' 30", and an indication of the capacity of the Yes west-coast band when it was willing to stretch out musically. Another environmentally attuned track, Wurzel dubs it 'a miracle of maths'. It begins with ascending, scale-like runs on bass, alongside descending treble sequences on keyboard. It is in 17/8, with three bars of five and an odd one of two. The melodic material is anthemic, and there is an 'as live' interlude. 'Silent Talking' (4' 00") is strong in a different way, eliding two distinct but complementary songs. Howe's guitar work here (again adapted via *Turbulence*) could and should have been given more room to breathe.

Another real highlight on *Union* is 'The More We Live – Let Go' (4' 51"), written by Chris Squire and Billy Sherwood. The concentrated, sombre harmony, supplemented by Anderson, combines with an expanding dynamic and several key changes to produce a compelling finale and a real sense of grandeur and ultimate fulfilment. The bass part is by Sherwood. Squire declined an opportunity to re-record it. This successful outing prefigured other fruitful collaborations from the pair, in *The Chris Squire Experiment*, the band Conspiracy and beyond.

'Angkor Wat' (5' 23"), referencing the largest ancient temple complex in the world, is unlike anything else in the Yes catalogue. Arising from an evocative, inviting vocal line from Anderson, it features a fabulously eerie, atmospheric keyboard sound collage (with Elias replacing Wakeman's effusions) and concludes with a moving recital of Cambodian poetry by Pauline Cheng.

The Yes dance/disco simulacrum 'Dangerous (Look in the Light of What You're Searching For)' has unsurprisingly attracted some criticism, but personally I really like it. Clocking in at 3' 36", it is almost a self-parody and pastiche, full of overwrought harmony, rhythmic twists and an off-the-edge finish. Great fun. 'Holding On' (5' 24"), on the other hand, has a resonant, searching atmosphere, with growling bass and clattering drums. It is a solid piece of writing and arranging. Then we have 'Evensong', an affecting miniature instrumental with a gamelan tone, featuring Bill Bruford on vibes and Tony Levin on bass. It arose from their duet in the *ABWH* tour. Another take from the same session was used by Levin for one of his solo outings.

The last track on *Union* is 'Take the Water to the Mountain'. This is a tune that suits Jon Anderson well, but only after the key change, when it moves up a gear. There was a missed chance here to allow Steve Howe to develop his guitar motifs into something suitably climactic. The Japanese album release features a further track, 'Give and Take'. This is a peppy little number, though, as Brian Wurzel comments, it "drops its ghost on a throwaway of three apologetic little notes." Perhaps this inability to bring ideas to full fruition is symptomatic of the band as as a whole at this time. *Union* has its moments, and is far better than the caustic criticism from within the band might allow, but, as Levin commented to Rok Podgrajšek afterwards:

> As you maybe would expect from a label like Arista, the goal seemed not to be to celebrate the great playing of those musicians, but to sell a lot of records.

It barely achieved that either, making no more nor less of a market impact (around 750,000 copies worldwide) than the *Anderson Bruford Wakeman Howe* record it succeeded. After touring, the eight-piece Yes Union line-up dissipated, leaving the west-coast band to make the next move.

Yesyears and 'America'

Yesyears is a career-spanning collection of music to date from Yes that was released as a four-disc box set on 6 August 1991. It is worth mentioning here because it contains several songs otherwise unreleased – among them the Netherlands stereo mix of Yes tackling Bernstein and Sondheim's 'Something's Coming' (7' 06"), 'Money' (3' 12") from the *Tormato* sessions, featuring a thoroughly forgettable Wakeman rant about allegedly paying too much tax under a Labour government, and Howe's 'Abilene', a B-side from the 'Don't Kill the Whale' single in August 1978. There is also Lennon and McCartney's 'I'm Down' (2' 31", live from the Roosevelt Stadium, NJ, in June 1976) and the anthemic ballad 'Love Conquers All', written by Chris Squire and Billy Sherwood, from the 1991 *Union* sessions, with Trevor Rabin singing the vocal line. These are all curiosities for the Yes listener, but there is nothing definitive to be mined.

One further inclusion of perhaps greater interest is a single edit of the reworking the band did in 1970 of Paul Simon's 'America', used in abbreviated form on *The New Age of Atlantic* compilation (1972), and then released complete in 1975 on the early years compilation, *Yesterdays*. The full version (10' 30") is a classic piece of Yes arranging, also including a short counter-pointed quotation on bass from the Leonard Bernstein tune of the same name. In particular, Howe's telescopic Gibson soloing projects the standard song into a whole new dimension of music. Some remember that Bruford recorded an early Mellotron part that Wakeman then overdubbed, though he recalls it differently. Squire, White and Howe play their hearts out on this track, and Anderson's alto voice retains the slightly smoky edge it had back in the late 1960s. The changes in time signature and long instrumental segments are characteristic of the band in the early 1970s, while the song's original repeat and fade ending are dropped. 'America' also appears on *The Ultimate Yes: 35th Anniversary Collection* (2003). The edited version was additionally included as a bonus track on the re-issue of *Close to the Edge*. A live version of the song features on 1996's *Keys to Ascension* (see below) as well as a performance from the final show of the 1970/71 tour, preceding the studio recording, on *The Word Is Live* (2005).

Talk

In interviews with Tim Morse and Chris Welch, Trevor Rabin has been keen to stress that the notion he operated as some kind of dictator within the group is wrong. Nevertheless, his all-encompassing talent in the studio, in music craft and in bringing committed compositions (rather than shadowy ideas) to the table shifted the agenda radically within Yes. The visible imprint resulting from this contribution was arguably as substantial in its own way as Jon Anderson's impact on 1970s incarnations of the band. During his 13 years with Yes (not counting the more recent Anderson / Rabin / Wakeman project from October

2016), Rabin undoubtedly gained "the right to rearrange how the story can be told", to quote from 'The Calling', the opening number on 1994's monumental *Talk* album. This influence is as deep and thoroughgoing as it is organic and subtle, notwithstanding some passionate arguments with producer Trevor Horn and others at times. The proof of this lies in that third full album from west-coast Yes, even though Anderson was, for the first time with Rabin, fully involved in composition from the outset.

More than any other studio recording from them, it is 1994's *Talk* that can be seen and heard as 'west-coast Yes' creating a musical flavour very much their own, yet one which also owes dues to the glories of the past. Here is that old Yes grandeur, variety and surprise translated into a cinematic, stadium rock sound – replete with a biting beat, swathes of textured colour, tempo changes, dynamic bursts, driving positivity, curious twists, underlying menace, melodic strength, balladic tenderness, metallic aggression and more. The *Talk* tour in the US and Japan, though not a great commercial success, confirmed these impressions with its cinemascopic force and intensity.

When I first heard the album, it was in the inauspicious surroundings of a London taxi cab. Returning from an overseas trip a few days after its release on 21st March 1994, I rushed out of the airport into a record store. All I had on me was a portable cassette player and headphones. So I purchased it on both tape and CD. I was intrigued to find out how a long-form composition from west-coast Yes would sound. As ever, the press preludes to the album spoke of a 'Close to the Edge' for the '90s. Not having heard any advance tapes, all I had to go on before encountering the final product was my own musical imagination, filtering early Yes through the very different impulses of the Rabin band. *Big Generator*, I reasoned, had come close to taking elements of pre-'71 Yes and processing it through the anthemic twists and turns provided by its new director's technical prowess. The impact, particularly on tracks such as 'I'm Running' and 'Shoot High, Aim Low', had been surprisingly convincing. It somehow sounded like a new Yes in a way *90125* had not. *Talk* would take this to the next level, perhaps?

The first thing to realise about this album is that it does not sit well with inferior sound reproduction. Painstakingly pioneered as a digital-only album on four Macs (this is some 25 years ago, remember) it aimed to achieve real depth and power. We now live in a time when there is little excuse for listening to music on tinny delivery systems. But that cassette in a cab was all I had at the time, and (foolishly, perhaps), having anticipated this moment for weeks, I was not going to wait another two hours for my first taste. What hit me first was a ferocious and rather obvious backbeat after the vocal harmonies that introduce 'The Calling'. I listened, then fast-forwarded in a stop-start way through the whole album. This was not what I had reckoned on at all. Yes always surprises. What has come before may shape what happens next, but not in any predictable way.

Talk kicks off with 'The Calling' (6' 52"), a forceful, extended FM-oriented song about seeking unity between human civilisations, and one built out of the opening guitar riff and vocal harmony (0:00–0:24). In the Japanese release a quiet, suspended interlude occurs at the midway point, but this is less than organic to the cumulative energy of the track. A different mood is conjured up by 'I Am Waiting' (7' 22"), which alternates between a delicate, pleading guitar motif and an exultant, climactic major key theme (00.27–1:14). It features some heart-wrenching singing from Anderson (4:45–4:55, "Highways, starways / Many ways to be open tonight"), is based on nakedly visceral emotional appeal, and ends as quietly as it began – but on a note not quite as unresolved as 'Hearts' (*90125*).

'Real Love' (8' 42") is inspired by the theoretical physics of Professor Stephen Hawking, who explores the origins and immensity of the universe from the very considerable limitations imposed on his own body by Motor Neurone Disease. Here Anderson links the physicality of the world to the quest for cosmic consciousness and the "love in the atoms" (Chelsea Marcantel). Chris Squire's rumbling, billowing bass is central to the construction of the song, along with the distant, off-key piano. There is a brooding intensity here, built on rock-hard foundations. The tension is released brashly on the loud, assertive 'State of Play' (4' 58"), which is in many respects 'Almost Like Love' (*Big Generator*) part two. Rabin's harmonised guitar call is rapidly joined by White's thumping drums and Squire's deep bass (possibly synthesised, as on much of the album) before Anderson breaks into the storm with acoustically conveyed stream-of-consciousness lyrics. There are two vocal themes, punctuated and joined by a siren-like, screaming guitar solo. The chaos of the world is both terrible and beautiful. But the response is in our hands: "No need to ask for help / It's in the love we breathe / Dancing in the new design – it's just a state of play." This is metal with energy and intelligence.

Over the years Yes have incorporated or adapted most styles of music. That includes country, which forms the basis of the unlikely inclusion on *Talk* of 'Walls', a radio song that Rabin co-wrote with Roger Hodgson. The former Supertramp frontman provides some backing vocals. A positively anthemic track that works well live, it is transfigured for a moment by Anderson's high range, spine-tingling interjection (3:31): "Oh, this indecision / Can break me down / Let it run to the river, tell me." A first take of the song was recorded in 1990 and is included on Trevor Rabin's demo album, *90124*. There is another dramatic change of mood with the meditative, questioning 'Where Will You Be' (6' 03"). This is a Rabin–Anderson collaboration very much on the latter's esoteric territory in its subject matter – reincarnation – and in its unpredictable lyrical shape. It features some exquisite guitar work from Rabin alongside White's tabla.

Endless Dream

However, the climax and summit of *Talk* is undoubtedly the lengthy (15'48") three-part suite, 'Endless Dream'. This is the west-coast band's version of the earlier Yes epics, using beautifully rounded vocal harmony and a range of instrumental ideas and motifs to achieve a panoramic sound building towards a gripping climax and a hauntingly delicate finale. After hearing this piece it makes total sense that Trevor Rabin went on to be an award-winning movie composer, because in so many respects the music is deeply filmic. It opens with the frenetic 1'56" instrumental, 'Silent Spring' (shades of Rachel Carson's apocalyptic environmental classic, published in 1962), starting with Rabin's (not Kaye's) fast, circular electric piano, thunderclap bass and drums, and then a 15/8 romp featuring heavy guitars and a howling Hammond organ.

Ending abruptly, a distant piano figure introduces the next section ('Talk'), which entails an unfolding conversational and dialogical lyric, starting with treated vocals and piano (1:57-3.45), before the main theme is introduced. A dystopian, effects-laden guitar growl and a lyrical attack on the greedy blandishments of televangelism punctuates the flow for a short while (5:16-6:22), before the main theme returns triumphantly and there is a dramatic key shift ahead of Anderson's re-entry: "It's the first time / Getting it / This life / First calling, in a silent spring." The programmed instrumental (7:21-9:15) has considerable range and texture. Anderson penetrates the looming uncertainty with a distant cry (9:17, "Coming in through the light...") before a brief, fractured reprise of the opening instrumental (9:26-10:05). The 'Talk' theme makes its final, decisive call, with Anderson's soaring counterpoint galvanising an unfolding, harmonised melodic line of incredible power: "When the world brings you down / Got to play this living game." By 13:49 the resurgent energy is spent, and the song segues into a deceptively calm, fluid parting rhythm. The final affirmation is both universal and personal ("For you are light / Inside your dreams / For you will find / That it's something that touches me." We are at sundown. But the final motion is a scratch ending. The shadow of death is not entirely excised.

The structure, power and harmonic resonance of 'Endless Dream' is remarkable, and in my view earns the piece a place among the Yes classics, despite its very different style. Talking to Tim Morse in 1995, Jon Anderson rated it alongside 'Close to the Edge' and 'Awaken'. Aficionados of the full-throttle '70s Yes might not agree, but there is something truly substantial and enduring about this long-form piece. Taking *Talk* as a whole, there was material that didn't make it, inevitably. Alan White mentioned 'Scarlet from the Tide' in 1993, but that has never appeared.

Forged unquestionably out of rock muscle, soundtrack structure and rich instrumentation, this album is surely the major statement from the Rabin-era Yes, and deserves its place in the varied history of the band. Its critical reception at the time was mixed, with *Rolling Stone* declining to reward the band for abandoning the "noodling" they were often (inaccurately) accused of, and William Ruhlmann inexplicably calling it "a disaster" on *AllMusic*. Retrospective assessment has been much kinder, rightly in my view.

Keys to Ascension

Rabin and Kaye decided to leave the band after the *Talk* album and the Japan tour in 1995, and the future of Yes was once again in doubt and up for grabs. Indeed, according to doyen biographer Chris Welch (2008) they were "[in] danger of slipping back into an obscurity more dark and profound than at any time in their history." Much as he had done after *Big Generator* in 1988, Jon Anderson therefore decided to "take the band towards the twenty-first century" by revisiting 'classic Yes' territory. The outcome, to the surprise of many, was the reappearance of the Anderson/Howe/Squire/Wakeman/White line-up, last seen on 1978's *Tormato*. This was galvanised by three live concerts at the art deco Freemont Theatre in San Luis Obispo, California, where Anderson was living. Aside from a patchily edited concert DVD (1996), the outcome of these gigs and a return to recording for the first time in some 20 years was a two-album project, *Keys to Ascension*, featuring a mix of live and new studio tracks, plus atmospheric 'Arches Mist' landscape artwork from Roger Dean. The first album was released on 28th October 1996, the second on 3rd November 1997, and a combination of the studio tracks, inelegantly entitled *Keystudio*, appeared on 21st May 2001. It is the latter that I will use to introduce the fresh material, which is clearly a conscious effort to revive the creative mojo of the '70s band, but with a '90s twist.

The standout tracks turned out to be the two long-form suites, 'That, That Is' (*Keys 1*) and 'Mind Drive' (*Keys 2*), in my view. We will return to these shortly. First let's consider the other five. 'Be the One' (the only other studio piece from *Keys 1*) is a strange mixture. The under-produced vocals and instrumentation of the first and third parts, with their pedestrian 4/4 and plodding chorus make this sound too much like a demo. But in the middle there is a gem. The 'Humankind' section, created by Anderson and Squire, features a superb climbing guitar sequence from Howe. Yes are truly back ... but then the magic disappears again.

'Foot Prints' begins with an unexpectedly gospel-style civil rights cry: "My eyes see the coming revolution/My eyes see the glory of the world." There is swing and syncopation in all this, driven by White's scattered drums patterns, before Squire introduces the 5/4 centrepiece bass blues riff (2:08) on his Tobias four-string, which was extended by four frets and tuned to C to enable it to go as low as the Tobias five-string. Proceeding through several phases, it is an intriguingly different song from a clearly revamped Yes.

Announced by a pair of six bell-like notes from Howe's guitar, 'Bring Me to the Power' (7' 23"), written with Anderson, references in its lyrics the title originally slated for what became *Talk*, namely 'the history of the future'. Victory Records soon squashed that idea, however! This song features what many would regard as Yes trademark shifts in tempo, dynamics and time signatures. It feels a little awkward at times, but also contains moments of rare beauty. Billy Sherwood's engineering (with Bill Smith and Tom Fletcher) and his production give a crisp, clean and well-differentiated finish. The layered vocals are a departure from the '70s sound and more a feature of the band in the '80s and especially the '90s and beyond. The instrumental coda from 6:12 is superbly skittish, as Wakeman's Moog dances over the top. With more work you sense this could be something really special.

'Children of Light' (7' 02") falls in two parts. The first, written jointly by Vangelis, utilises a rapping, modern Romantic poem called 'Distant Thunder' that Jon Anderson first employed for his page in the *Union* tour programme in 1991. It again picks up the theme of human rights, dignity and aspiration beyond a world of greed and war. The *Keystudio* album features a different mix from *Keys* 2, with Wakeman's dense, classical style synth introduction, 'Lightening', re-introduced. The song was performed by Anderson, ahead of its inclusion on the album, at a Mother's Day concert in the USA on 12th May 1996. The second section (from 3:58), 'Lifeline', is shaped by Howe's steel guitar and is a classic piece of Yes instrumental arranging, dripping with emotional power. Meanwhile, 'Sign Language' (3' 28"), which is also fully instrumental, is probably one of Yes's least known tunes. But it is definitely worthwhile, influenced by light classical music, and featuring Wakeman's orchestral synth, piano, and Howe's crystalline semi-acoustic playing. The guitars featured on the *Keys* project, incidentally, are 6- and 12-string electric and acoustics, steel and pedal steels, and a 5-string bass.

That, That Is

This leaves us with the two longest tracks. 'That, That is' (19' 15") falls into seven interlinked sections. In place of Anderson's usual mystical themes, which were in danger of becoming dislocated and clichéd by this point, the song material wrestles with poverty, inner city decay and the psychological pressures this produces. It is at once fatalistic (as the title might suggest) and optimistic (as we would expect from Anderson). One thing it is not, despite the dark theme, is political in any engaged way. Of all the material I have re-listened to in writing *Solid Mental Grace*, I would say that this piece is the one that stands out as a 'lost classic' from Yes. It is unusual and slightly left field in every way, attempting to forge a new language out of inherited grammar and vocabulary. Its musical syntax is distinct. Highlights include Howe's acoustic guitar at the beginning (0:16–3:17), trailing Wakeman's fairground synth, and the primal chant and drums section (3:35–4:24) leading into the first vocal theme (4:25–7:05). The next vocal motif ("That talk is just a worry and a worry") introduces a plaintiff, melancholy note. Then at 8:42, the mood shifts again, as the same lyrics are taken up almost as a protest song (9:04–11:15). The "All in all" section recaptures a sense of hope in the midst of struggle. From 13:40–14:20 there is a burst of optimism ("This time is meant to be") that falls back into the early chant and on to a recapitulation ("These days are just a worry to the children of the world / How did heaven begin?"). The drive to resolution begins at 15:20, as Howe's Gibson pivots us upstream (15:58–17:55) and Anderson ("Live for the breaking freedom / Just let it come through") returns to hammer the hope home, assisted by White's drumming at the end. An extraordinary finale.

Mind Drive

If 'That, That Is' sounds like nothing Yes had delivered before, 'Mind Drive' (18' 40"), one of nine pieces lasting over 18 minutes from the band over their career, echoes back closer to the *Going for the One* era, though it is less polished than 'Awaken', say. It was originally an instrumental concept that the band XYZ, which featured Chris Squire, Alan White and Jimmy Page, wrote and demoed in 1981. It was later incorporated into a drum duet involving Alan White and Bill Bruford on the *Union* tour. This suite saw it to fruition. The instrumental opening, beginning again with Wakeman on synths and Howe on pinpoint acoustic guitar, joined by Chris Squire's tuneful bass, is immensely strong (0:00–1:59). It is a high-end figure from Squire that marks the transition into the XYZ drum pattern, with a shifting 7/8 time signature (2:00–3:56).

Anderson comes in off the beat with an opening verse that is almost declaimed rather than sung. Howe emphasises the melody (4:30–4:45) and Anderson recapitulates. By far the weakest part of the suite, repeated twice more (the first time at 7:50ff), is the "They will bring you rain" section. It is mixed too high – a real contrast in dynamics is needed here – and is far too twee. A heavier feel is restored by Squire's bass at 5:45, and the extended 'Mind Drive' motif comes in for the first time. Howe's acoustic and flamenco break (8:28) marks the halfway point of the piece, weaving into another new vocal theme from Anderson. Squire's scale-like descending bass (10:17) and White's playful cymbals (10:58) give way to a fearsome synth lead from Wakeman (11:21–12:23) as the concluding instrumental themes are introduced, prior to a vocal reprise and summary (12:25–13:44).

The propulsive ending of 'Mind Drive' (15:15) is foregrounded by Howe's guitar and Squire's thundering bass until Wakeman's Moog (16:35) dives in, and the whole instrumental mêlée hurtles into a breakneck finale (17:15). It is a moment in Yes music you will either love or loathe. For me it is in the former category, until the music tumbles over the edge (17:44) in a dramatic downward bass *diminuendo* that partially resolves itself on a low E and then on a fragment of what sounds like synth fairground music – just to dispel the grandeur of what has gone before and to stop us all from taking ourselves *too* seriously. Overall 'Mind Drive' is a success, but with enough unevennesses to make it something of a 'work in progress' that improved with (regrettably limited) live performances.

Chapter 10
Turn Around and Remember
(1998–2004)

If you ask me, music is the language of memory.

– Jodi Picoult

The period from 1991 to early 1997 marked three experimental transitions in the development of Yes music after the 1970s heydays and the commercial success of the 1980s west-coast based band. *Union,* despite its shortcomings, established a template for a '90s Yes, combining sound sources from the classic and modern band, and beyond. *Talk* brought the Rabin project to a natural and (in terms of scope and sound) widescreen conclusion. And the *Keys to Ascension* recordings in 1996 and 1997 pushed the last 1970s line-up as far as it could go in both re-capitulating and modernising its artistic approach. Meanwhile, further changes were on the way. Rick Wakeman's latest tenure with Yes did not last beyond the Freemont concerts and the studio sessions, for apparently logistical reasons, though with an element of personality mixed in. A new management company, the Left Bank Organisation, however, was keen for the band to tour again from late 1997 into 1998, and to have an album ready for those purposes.

If Yes was to continue in 1998 and beyond, it seemed it would have to do so with a new approach to the place of keyboards in the mix and a new sense of direction. Billy Sherwood, a multi-instrumentalist, composer, producer and Chris Squire collaborator, formerly of progressive band World Trade, had toured as an additional guitar and keyboard player with the *Talk* band in 1994. He had also engineered and produced *Keys to Ascension 2*, to everyone's general satisfaction. He and Squire now saw the need to press Yes forward again, in a project that became the *Open Your Eyes* album, released right at the end of 1997 but also toured throughout 1998. In the midst of this, Igor Khoroshev, an extraordinarily talented but volatile keyboard player from Russia, came on board, having met Jon Anderson through Carl Jacobson of the Cakewalk software house. He arrived just in time to play on a couple of *Open Your Eyes* tracks, with the album awkwardly appearing on the back of *Keys 2*, due to the strange record company and commercial decisions that have plagued Yes in their latter years.

Open Your Eyes

Like *Union*, the *Open Your Eyes* album, subsequently seen by some as a bit of a 'filler' in the catalogue, has not achieved a great deal of acceptance among either Yes aficionados or the wider community of music critics. Like the two albums that succeeded it, it can be understood partially as an act of remembering and rejoining prominent elements in Yes music, to see if, out of this admixture, a new recipe for the band could emerge. Sherwood fused the refreshing production values of *Keys to Ascension 2* and the intensely layered sound texture of *Union* into the generation of *Open Your Eyes*, which curated existing material from Anderson and Howe, as well as his own writing with Squire from their work in the band Conspiracy. The result was less than even, and perhaps too driven by the record company's desire for radio airplay, but its major components certainly offered some sense of the new sound Yes appeared to be searching for. This was neither the grandiose stadium rock of *Talk*, nor the retro-style of *Keys*, nor the indigestion and incompatibilities of *Union*, but a modern progressive rock aesthetic residing in shorter-form pieces and a reconditioning of the original vision of bringing vocal harmony and instrumental dexterity together. To achieve this it might have been advisable to stick to around 40 minutes of music. In the end, the album came out at over 74 minutes, with a total of eleven songs and a hidden 16' 10" ambient track entitled 'The Source'.

'New State of Mind' (6' 00") sets the scene with its muscular vocals, swooping melody, bold harmony and Khoroshev's keyboard drop. It manages to sound simultaneously simple and sophisticated. Next up is title track 'Open Your Eyes' (5' 14") – originally 'Wish I Knew' from Conspiracy, and featuring Steve Porcaro on keyboards. This has a notable hook and works well in concert. It showcases the strongly melodic approach that Billy Sherwood sought to bring to the band at this juncture.

At one point the album was to have been named after the third track, 'Universal Garden', which might have given the project a rather different sensibility. This is one of the most successful pieces on the album, combining coherent song material with an updated orchestral feel and a delayed measure that gives it a spaciousness one can readily associate with Yes in any era. Another strong contribution musically is the slick, modern and sinewy 'Fortune Seller' (5' 00"), which again seems to pack a punch larger than its modest size might indicate. Igor Khoroshev's organ solo is particularly successful here. In between these two is sandwiched 'No Way We Can Lose' (4' 56"), a tunefully anthemic number that the band played just twice live, once in Connecticut and once with a school choir at the Universal Amphitheatre in California.

Chris Squire's tongue-in-cheek 'Man in the Moon' (4' 41') features a gorgeously nagging guitar hook from Howe, noticeably missing on the Conspiracy original. Again, its principal virtue is melody, along with wry humour. 'Wonderlove' (6' 06") and 'Love Shine' (4' 38") are song titles no one ever really anticipated on a Yes album. The saccharine texture of the tunes has also earned them some measure of disdain from longer-term fans. But they are extremely well crafted and contain some good writing and arranging. One feels that with more input from Steve Howe (who felt marginalised in this project), more time for development, and different titles, they could have both retained the melodic attraction and fitted better with the Yes legacy. 'From the Balcony' (2' 43") is a miniature duet from Howe and Anderson. It comes across as gentle, charming but also a little naïve – despite, according to its composer, containing a lyrical dig at past management ups and downs! At one London concert, on 5th March 1998, a cellist from the London Philharmonic Orchestra, Susanne Beer, joined the duo for an amplified version of the song.

The penultimate piece, 'Somehow Someday' (4' 47") has a distinctly Celtic flavour and repackages motifs that originally appeared on Jon Anderson's solo albums *Animation* ('Boundaries', 1982), and especially *The Promise Ring* (1997). The attempt to 'Yessify' it produced mixed reactions. The final track on the album is the forceful 'The Solution' (5' 26"), which pulls all the stops out vocally and instrumentally. It is almost macho in its tension and assertiveness, with twists, turns and contrasts galore. It also appears to be something of a statement about the predicament of Yes at this time, referencing 'Roundabout' (1971) the 'round and round' motion of 1978's *Tormato*, and a message to listeners, "Giving in, giving out / Do the best you can do / Giving in, giving out / It's all up to you." This was indeed the best the band could offer in limiting circumstances by 1998, and it clearly posed more questions than it answered. Again, the faults are easy to spot. But perhaps it is also worth stepping back with hindsight to consider some of its stronger features. 'New State of Mind', 'Universal Garden', 'Fortune Seller' and 'The Solution' were all group collaborations, Billy Sherwood has since confirmed, and show the benefits of that.

The Ladder

The eighteenth studio album from Yes, *The Ladder*, was recorded early in 1999 at Armoury Studios in Vancouver, Canada, and released on 20th September that year. Though *Open Your Eyes* had not produced musical harmony or consensus within the band, being seen as a necessity rather than a virtue overall, the actual chemistry of the group seemed to be working reasonably well. The 1997 and 1998 tours in more intimate venues had brought Yes closer to their audience. Igor Khoroshev was capable of delivering the keyboard sound of the band from any era with little apparent effort and some panache. Amid the touring they agreed to work with veteran 'classic rock' producer Bruce Fairbairn, and to allow him to help the shape the new album. Tragically, he died just before it was completed, but it definitely bears his stamp.

Once again, there was an attempt to draw on trademarks from the 1970s, but to offer something more accessible to bridge the two previous, contrasting decades of Yes music. Having tasted the big time from 1983 to 1985, there were some in the group – perhaps especially Squire and Anderson – who could not let go of the idea that Yes could once again be popular and acclaimed. It was probably always an illusion, and tipped the band towards commercial elements in their sound that fulfilled neither the wishes of inherited audiences nor the capacity to draw in fresh appreciators. But in spite of that, *The Ladder*, again with a Roger Dean cover and inferences of Yoko Ono's London art installation (where you ascend rungs and see the word 'Yes' at the apex) contained some strong material, albeit far from the artistic heights the band had achieved in a different time and space.

Fairbairn was keen to get people working together, rather than dialing in some of their parts from afar, as had happened once more on *Open Your Eyes*. This made a real difference. *The Ladder* is coherent as a musical statement in ways its immediate predecessor is not. There are three tracks that particularly stand out from the rest for me. The opener, 'Homeworld (The Ladder)', expanded to 9' 32", was written in loose collaboration with video game developer Relic Entertainment and publisher Sierra Games. It focuses on a science fiction idea involving survivors of an embattled civilisation searching for a new home. Musically it is very much in progressive/classic rock territory, with bass, guitar and keys climbing the scales towards a summit that gives way to a disarmingly simple (in Yes terms almost simplistic) acoustic and vocal ending from Anderson accompanied by Khoroshev's piano. The two never did complete their mooted *True Me, True You* album project, incidentally. But Khoroshev's fine solo CD, *Piano Works* (1999) is clearly indicative of his capacity and leanings. Strains of the Russian Romantics (Tchaikovsky, Rachmaninov and Prokofiev) can be heard throughout. As on *Open Your Eyes*, Welch (2008) reports, Khoroshev wanted to play a Hammond B-3 organ. In the end he had to employ an organ simulator, since the processing sound of the Hammond bled into Alan White's drum tracks.

The second song on *The Ladder*, 'It Will Be a Good Day (The River)' (4' 54"), is a ravishingly beautiful example of Yes taking a popular song form and arranging it into something altogether larger and lusher. Howe's Steinberger figure (1:41–1:47) is particularly irresistible. Khoroshev provides a wide-screen orchestral synth sound and Squire's bass tastefully pulls the whole together. It is a wonderful piece of work in its own right, even though very far from the likes of *Relayer*, on which four of the protagonists on *The Ladder* played, and which for some of us helps define the essence of this group. The moral is to let the music speak for itself, not to press it through the lens of something other.

Much the same could be said for the next three tracks, which segue together and are seen by some as constituting an 'African trilogy', though the sound sources are Latin and Caribbean as well as from African and Western pop. 'Lightning Strikes' (4' 35") begins with Mellotron flutes and part of a solo borrowed from the opening of 'Phenomenal Cat' (1968) by The Kinks. It is a joyous dance tune with a cute little bass wiggle in the middle. At first I disliked it intensely, so far is it from any idea I had of Yes. But, once more, it is always worth listening beyond the point of having your prejudices confirmed. I agree with critic Jason Warburg, however, that Jon Anderson's tendency towards whimsy, New Age cliché and "airy optimism" was by this stage doing Yes few favours. The autodidact striving of his early lyrics had latterly been replaced by easy resort to a range of nature metaphors and analogies that were too easily parodied in online 'Yes lyric generators'. Meanwhile, 'Can I?' (1' 32") provides an indigenous chant-like bridge (similar to one in 'That, That Is') and quotes from 'We Have Heaven' from *Fragile* (1971). It bleeds into the bubbling cauldron of 'Face to Face' (5' 43"). Here, hints at the melodies and instruments of the South African township are taken up into a pulsating, pleasing 7/4 tune that is unlike anything Yes have ventured before. It is commendable in that respect as well as for its sheer *joie de vivre*.

It was an undeniably brave decision to go in this uncharted direction for Yes. Less justifiable from that point of view, at least in my opinion, is the inclusion of Anderson's love song to his second wife, Jane Luttenburger, 'If Only You Knew' (5' 43"). Like 'Love Will Find a Way', it is a perfectly well presented and memorable pop song, but something of a baffling and unnecessary choice for this band. The singer was evidently calling the shots on this, and the commercial leanings are clear. 'To Be Alive (Hep Yadda)' is more of that seemingly impossible thing, catchy and danceable Yes (5' 07"). It has distinct echoes of Anderson's *In the City of Angels* (1988) solo work. 'The Messenger' (5' 13") features a restrained reggae feel and some nifty bass maneouvres. It is a tribute to Bob Marley, along the lines of a suggestion from Fairbairn, apparently.

Another quite personal statement from Anderson comes in the last track on *The Ladder*, 'Nine Voices', which is based on The Longest Walk, a spiritual trek across the USA that took place in 1978. It was organised by the American Indian Movement (AIM) to call for tribal sovereignty. Chris Welch reports (2008) that Anderson had befriended one of the participants, Long Walker. He subsequently wrote the piece about nine tribe members singing together to "bring forgiveness into the world". It is touching and effective, and was movingly played by Anderson and Howe at Bruce Fairbairn's funeral. On a pedantic note, nine voices do not constitute a dialogue, but we understand the intention! The reference to North Africa is also a little out of place. Howe's Portuguese 12-string and emulated sitar sound, together with White's tabla and Squire's bass pedals, lend a quirky multicultural dimension to the instrumentation. All part of its strange and eccentric charm.

This leaves two important pieces on the album that reflect the band working together more organically. 'Finally' (6' 02") falls into two parts. The first is an urgent song that almost trips over itself in its attempt to make its point, lurching into action with no attempt at a prelude. It is perhaps a little too rushed, though given the theme of the lyrics, one appreciates that this is precisely the idea. Here is Yes biting the music industry hand that feeds it, with Howe delivering a blow in his own way, through a short guitar solo (2:00–2:25). The real payoff, however, is the extended coda – "I can feel the rain coming / I can feel the love coming / I can feel the earth moving." The combination of instruments (from 3:23) and the slow, dynamically constructed development to an understated conclusion and acoustic ending is for me one of many truly spine-tingling moments in the history of Yes music.

Last, but definitely not least, we have 'New Language' (9:19), the track that – as it happens – most surely checks the expected progressive rock boxes. We open with Khoroshev's church organ, actually delivered on Yamaha keyboards and doubled by Howe on lead guitar and punctuated by drums and bass (0:00–0:37). This sequence tips into a wildly swinging group jam in 11/8, joined by some fabulous Hammond B-3 playing. It rocks like crazy and is very clever without being over self-conscious: Yes instrumental prowess at its best. The song itself enters at 2:07, full of wry self-deprecation from Anderson, as in 'Going for the One' (1977). He tells us that, "I speak from some sort of protection of learning / Even though I make it up as I go on." The 'new language' is an attempt to reflect a whole range of emotions and feelings through the prism of love. There is a new vocal theme at 3:20 – "Vision is coming so fast / I can't stop myself", and again at 3:52 – "Is there something that I'm supposed to see?" We then move on into an increasingly dramatic reprise (4:24–6:16) before Steve Howe's superb solo, recalling shades of jazz great Jim Hall (6:45–7:28). This is a section I can listen to again and again, harking back to Howe's work in the early 1970s, but with a different, updated guitar aesthetic. From 7:40–7:57 we are momentarily transported back to *Tales from Topographic Oceans*. Then the song we know so well re-enters and climaxes before a really well judged little instrumental coda (8:45), integrating past fragments into its concluding statement. 'New Language' is by far the most effective and cogent piece of music on *The Ladder,* and along with – perhaps surprisingly – 'It Will Be A Good Day' is for me its lasting legacy. Again, however, Yes leave us with a sense that there is more to come.

Magnification

In the end a further two years elapsed before Yes got back into the studio purposefully. By that time Igor Khoroshev's star had risen and fallen, though not on account of the music. On the otherwise superlative 'Masterworks' tour of the US in 2000, which I was privileged to see, the Russian keyboard player allowed his ego to run away with him and his various appetites. He ended up being sacked from the band over sexual assault allegations. It was a real tragedy, because in many respects he was an ideal figure behind the keyboards for Yes. He could handle the different styles of Kaye, Wakeman, Moraz and Downes perfectly, and brought his own licks and expression to the mix. I wondered about the possibility of a new 'classic Yes' with Khoroshev on board ... but then he was gone, and the process of the band's continual, uncertain and unfinished re-invention continued – as if they were in search of a song or symphony that could make itself hearable in fragments, but could never quite be found as a whole.

Over the spring and summer of 2001, in an unexpected twist, Yes decided to record a new studio album, *Magnification*, with supplementary orchestral arrangements taking the place of keyboards. It was a bold move, echoing what they had done with their second album, *Time and a Word* (1970), but with a degree of professionalism and technological capacity unheard of 31 years earlier. The album was recorded and mixed using Pro Tools, with producer Tim Weidner. Larry Groupé, who conducted the San Diego Symphony Orchestra, completed the orchestral arrangements in consultation with the band. I was immensely sceptical when I first heard about this, but was eventually won over by aspects of the album, and even more so by the ensuing tour, which was a real highlight in Yes history – especially when the band came to Europe and were accompanied not by scratch orchestras in each city, but by Harvey Keitel and the vigorously youthful European Festival Orchestra. The effort to once again create something resonant but also fresh on *Magnification* is reflected in the deep space cover by Bob Cesca, with an unadorned version of the organic Roger Dean Yes logotype.

Thinking of distinctive experiences that shape our hearing of music, I started to listen to the *Magnification* album on the train

Chapter 10 Turn Around and Remember • 147

from London to a conference at the University of Birmingham the day after it was released in the UK. The date was, in US notation, 9/11. I still have the rail ticket. By lunchtime I was watching with horror at what was unfolding at the Twin Towers in New York. What prefigured and followed those events (with even more telling and terrible consequences for millions of people in the Middle East and across the globe) lends added poignancy to the theme of the album, which is how to magnify good in the world and minimise that which shrinks or defaces human beings and the human spirit.

Magnification's ten pieces open with the title track (7' 16"), which 'swings with strings', as one fellow listener put it to me. The impact of working with an orchestra can certainly be heard to have consequences for the instrumentalists in the band, with White especially adapting his drum texture to the surroundings. This piece segues into 'Spirit of Survival' (6' 02"), a mini-epic that begins with Anderson's telling words: "In this world / the gods have lost their way." They certainly had in 2001, and on many other occasions throughout human history. Steve Howe came into the end of this project on the back of his own *Natural Timbre* (2001) album, and so brought with him a renewed stock of ideas about the role of the acoustic guitar. He provides the bridge into the first verse, to Squire's bouncing bass, and to the flashes and stabs of orchestral power that illuminate this track. 'Give Love Each Day' (7' 44") is not a particularly inviting title for the fourth song, but it is a solid and beautiful piece in other respects. Groupé wrote the 2' 06" orchestral prelude. The transition to the lyrical content is a single bass note from Squire (2:13). The music, interweaving and developing the vocals, has a filmic quality again. The chorus, which is also the title, does not actually arrive until 7:02. It all fits together surprisingly well.

In a quite different and more disposable way, 'Don't Go' (4' 27") was obviously Eagle/Beyond Music's nod in the direction of that essentially un-Yes-like entity, a single. It is a cute tune and story, borne early on by megaphone rather than vocoder. The young women of the European Festival Orchestra seemed to enjoy it, but in the overall flow of Yes music it is fairly forgettable, as is the sentimental 'Soft As a Dove' (2' 17") and – after a fine acoustic introduction by Howe – the lachrymose 'We Agree' (6' 30"). These are three pieces of music that I personally find difficult to spend too much time with, and to associate with the Yes legacy, but I am pleased if others hear and see them differently. They exemplify quite a bit of what can go wrong when a rock band gets entangled with an orchestra, an issue which I will refer to from another, more analytical, angle later on. It took me a little while to adjust to the very last track, 'Time is Time' (2' 09"), too. But I am glad that I did. It has strong echoes of early Yes and their brushes with the pre-*Sergeant Pepper* Beatles. In this case the inspiration is George Harrison, who coincidentally and sadly died while Yes were touring *Magnification*. You can hear the ex-Beatle in almost every groove. This track is simple but effective, and a decidedly non-pretentious way to sign off an album and project with a grand scale about it.

The other three pieces on *Magnification* are for me its highlights, along with 'Spirit of Survival'. First, 'Can You Imagine' (2' 59") is a fine testimony to the late Yes co-founder and bassist Chris Squire. It would have been wonderful to hear this song as part of the tributes to the great man during the 2016/17 tours. Unusually, the song features Squire on lead vocals and Anderson on backing vocals. It was originally recorded as a demo in 1981 for the proposed XYZ band featuring Squire, White and Jimmy Page, formerly of Led Zeppelin.

On the other hand, the curious expanded ballad 'In the Presence Of' (10' 24") came from a passage that Alan White was playing almost casually on a piano in the studio. Jon Anderson noticed it and expressed the desire to develop it further for the album. It was therefore composed in outline several years before this recording. The lyrics do not scan easily; but that has often been a feature of Anderson's lyrical and vocal work, stretching both the line and the melody to their limits in order to produce something different or contextually effective. The CD specifies four sections – Deeper, Death of Ego, True Beginner, and Turn Around and Remember. The finale is my favourite part of the song, but, like other notable highs within Yes's music, also acquires its significance from what precedes it. The long coda emerges (7:00) out of a broodingly intense bass scale developed by Howe's searching steel guitar, pizzicato strings, and finally drums. White starts to stretch the tempo at 8:01 and again at 8:40. But it is Howe's steel guitar that brings the whole section together triumphantly, with the orchestra accompanying. A piece of unalloyed magnificence on *Magnification,* it is almost concerto like in its style and impact. The very last word is a receding, wiry harmonic from Squire's Rickenbacker.

Dreamtime and after
Then there is 'Dreamtime', the longest track (10' 46"), which starts with a flamenco motif on Howe's Spanish guitar and then almost immediately takes off into a piece of music that could have been a film soundtrack (0:13), marked at both ends of the spectrum by the contrast and interweaving of Squire's bass, the guitar, textural strings and a lead violin. The orchestra and bass guitar double to stab the instrumental section into a calculated climax. Anderson's high, clear voice cuts through the strings at 1:40. Then at 2:05, tuned percussion, bass and orchestra rip into a new, faster riff. Although there are many ways in which I feel the term 'orchestral rock' has been abused and misused in the recent past, this section merits the appellation. The tumbling melody and harmony bears itself out up to "Talk among your one true self now / Forever, Forever" (3:50), before another funky, swinging, counterpointed instrumental theme tips over into a dreamy space-rock sequence (4:17–5:06) This is segued back into a further vocal climax by the Spanish Guitar. The woodwind breaks into an urgent flurry (5:55) and the previous

spacey sequence reprises, this time alongside some equally spacey lyrics. At 7:34, Squire's swooping bass brings in the orchestra, Howe's Gibson, a fugal string theme and a descending, stabbing finale. The coda is entirely orchestral, again provided by Groupé, who is effectively the fifth member of the group at this stage. It is a gorgeous piece of writing – Copland, Bernstein, Bartók: it's all in there. Another important and completely 'different' piece of Yes music, 'Dreamtime' utilises and leans on the orchestra in a way that *Time and a Word* failed to do. A fitting *dénouement*.

So where did these three quite different albums, *Open Your Eyes*, *The Ladder* and *Magnification* end up leaving Yes in the new millennium? In strong, positive, melodic territory, for sure. With glimpses of past glories etched into a sometimes uneven and uncertain musical landscape. With changing personnel, a host of ideas, a range of possibilities but also no definite sense of direction. Also with tensions between the commercial and artistic leanings of the band. That has been the story of Yes and its music ever since the different paths mapped by *Talk* on the one hand and *Keys to Ascension* on the other. There is much to be mined from this era, and several passages and pieces that give an abiding insight into who and what Yes continues to be into the twenty-first century. But there is no sense of resolution or arrival, so there is little point in looking for one. Just enjoy what's there, leave the rest.

Chapter 11
Along the Edge
(2005–2011)

> When people insist they like 'all kinds of music', that usually means that they really like no kinds of music.
>
> – Chuck Klosterman

While Yes's twentieth studio album, *Fly From Here,* certainly did not lay to rest longstanding disagreements about what constitutes the "essence" of Yes music, the album did and does offer more than a few clues about some of its most enduring traits. In spite of considerable investment in extended musical forays, for example, Yes's output predominantly revolves around song form. Likewise, though there is always plenty of instrumental prowess and complexity in the mix, vocal harmony landscapes the terrain the band operates on at many of its highest points.

Preparing for take-off

From the outset, the task of putting together up to an hour's worth of new and worthy Yes music in 2011 was always going to be challenging. The huge effort that had gone into 2001's *Magnification* had failed to produce the fresh breakthrough in critical and audience appreciation that some in and around the band had hoped for. Further personnel ins and outs followed. A reformed 'classic' line-up mostly pleased in concert, but did not produce any new material. Moreover, when Trevor Horn linked up again with Chris Squire in 2010, Yes as a music producing and performing outfit had been in hiatus for over five years – the longest period of its existence.

In other respects, too, the auguries were less than promising. The 2008–9 'In the Present' tour, though it unearthed and re-polished some rare Yes gems, had once again concentrated on extrapolating from past glories rather than developing original musical ideas. The introduction of Benoît David (vocals) and Oliver Wakeman (keyboards) produced uncharitable accusations from some quarters – those who still cared – that the band had effectively declined into a weak imitation of itself. Despite hopeful noises to the contrary, especially from the ever-restless Steve Howe, collective creativity seemed to have ebbed. As far as many were concerned Yes was effectively dissipated and off the 'new music' radar for good. Attention had turned to other, extra-curricula solo or collaborative ventures involving the Yes *alumni*.

But there was another dynamic to all this, which Horn, drafting in long-time ally Geoff Downes behind the keyboards, was able to help the band pick up on and take forward. A significant degree of internal harmony had already been restored as a result of younger, relatively even-tempered musicians coming into the setup – as well as invigorating energy. The Howe / Squire / White / David / Oliver Wakeman line-up had offered different, interesting insights into the *Drama*-era material, especially. The embers of productive desire were still there, it seemed. But it was not clear how they could be transformed into a new, cogent aural statement adequate to the task of re-establishing Yes as a going musical concern.

Fly From Here is both original and derivative. It sources material from over thirty years ago (the title song, and other material), but then uses it to pull together a picture of how Yes is, how it performs, and how it works in the now. That proved a sensible combination in the circumstances. It referenced the past unapologetically, but still managed to produce a pleasingly unpredictable present. The shorter components prove listenable (if not altogether memorable), but there is also something more connective and ambitious at play. The roots of Yes in melodic rock soil are evident, but also the inclination to employ far more subtle or adventurous ideas from a much wider musical palette, and to implement them through a range of textures, sound structures and recording techniques – while holding on to something that is identifiably the shared output of five musicians (six if you include Horn at the controls and adding backing vocals, as is the case here).

Correspondingly, the more obvious mistakes from Yes's chequered past are avoided. In particular, the band worked together with the producer in one location, rather than swapping sound fragments across the oceans and then leaving it to an army of largely unseen and unmet collaborators to rework them (as happened with *Union*). On this album only Gerard Johnson's additional keyboards on 'The Man You Always Wanted Me To Be' were provided "at a distance", because he contributed them to an earlier demo for material that was previously slated to appear on Squire's elusive second solo album. Then it got brought into the 2010–11 Yes sessions.

Much could be said about Trevor Horn in relation to this project. His technical abilities and sensibilities speak for themselves. The reliance on MIDI and the Pro Tools digital audio workstation will not be to everyone's taste. But the processing and editing is not as obtrusive on this album as on some of its predecessors, and the resulting sound, while multi-layered, is clean and often closely microphoned, in order to bring out the distinctive instrumental 'voices'. One especially interesting decision was to bring Geoff Downes on keys – replacing Oliver

Wakeman part way though the 2010-11 recording sessions. It was to prove an enduring choice.

The contribution of Benoît David also came into its own during the realisation of *Fly From Here*. With advice and some further training, David's singing had strengthened and improved since he arrived on the Yes scene in 2008, though he subsequently experienced severe vocal and pitch problems on the July US mini-tour and contracted laryngitis in December 2011. The impact of this produced a plethora of unflattering YouTube concert clips.

Days of future past?
The 23' 43" length 'Fly From Here' is unlike most of Yes's other extended 18-minute-plus works. Rather than presenting, elaborating and reprising a set of thematic material, it is essentially a suite of songs interwoven with instrumental ideas and sharing some melodic and harmonic features. There is development, for sure. But several of the six sections (Overture / We Can Fly / Sad Night At The Airfield / Madman At The Screens / Bumpy Ride / We Can Fly - Reprise) also have stand-alone qualities, especially the first three. Comments from Alan White and Geoff Downes following the release of the *Fly From Here* album suggest that the question of whether the tracks should be individuated or combined into a larger whole remained on hold throughout the recording process, right up until the final stages.

The 'Overture' (which in parts bears some family resemblance to the more frantic 'Silent Spring', the opening section of 1994's 'Endless Dream') introduces its initial theme on processed piano, then adds a full staccato statement of the first theme before clipping it further when introducing bass, drums and a simple contrapuntal riff (0:28) – which is then picked up on guitar and orchestral keyboards. The segue into a related new theme (1:15) sets out, in abbreviated form, one of the melodies developed more fully in 'Part III: Madman At The Screens', which in turn elaborates and expands upon the principal 'Overture' material. In turn, Part III includes a variation on the secondary theme introduced in the latter half of 'Part II: Sad Night at the Airfield', based upon the second demo track on the re-released *Adventures in Modern Recording*. Horn and Downes are the composers for each of these sections. The music is, as Steve Howe suggested in a March 2011 interview with Victoria Advocate Live, "neat, stylish, [and] clever".

'Part I: We Can Fly' is the heart of the suite – a song that emerges quietly from one of three atmospheric electronic interludes that punctuate the piece as a whole, accumulating and extending towards a majestic, anthemic chorus. The piano element at the beginning is in the clustered chordal American style exemplified by Alan White's introduction to 'In the Presence Of' (*Magnification*) or Trevor Rabin on *Talk*. The material is developed and projected instrumentally and vocally before drawing breath again in the segue into Part III. Benoît David's singing is resonant, high, well articulated and interestingly phrased. Steve Howe's telescopic, angular guitar work blends and contrasts effectively with the sweeter tone of Geoff Downes' keys and some rich vocal harmonies. This section of the piece is well anchored by shifting rhythms and harmonising bass – either a ten-string, or possibly an 8-string octave overdub, with ample use of pedals. Rhythmically, the link is in 5/4 while the underlying structure is 4/4.

The haunting, melancholic but satisfyingly beautiful approach of 'Part II: Sad Night At The Airfield' is set in motion by Howe's delicate acoustic guitar. Like the two previous sections, it possesses integrity in itself, while fitting well in the song sequence, and hinting at the 'fly from here' theme (1:49). Arcs of piano, a steady rhythm and waves of sumptuous synth frame the two intersecting vocal sections, with the growing contrast in dynamics evened out by the appearance of a warm, rounded high-end bass restatement of the principal motif (3:22) – a five-note figure that alternates between the instruments, eventually pulling together (4:48) in a mellifluous but not overstated climax ("turn your life around ... I watch the stars"). The texturing and layering is exquisite and the melodic lines are memorable.

'Part III: Madman At the Screens' creates an altogether different atmosphere. A dense, sunken and slightly dissonant electronic theme sees the reappearance of the processed piano from the Overture, followed by a re-statement of the riff in lyrical form against a flattened acoustic. White's drums, Howe's electric guitar licks and a rapid vocal duet in music theatre style propel the section forwards into the storm clouds – with bursts of snare serving as a warning, but the overall song persists and grows, nonetheless. The instrumental work has drive and urgency, recalling some of the soundscapes on 1978's *Tormato*, before organ and piano re-introduce a sense of calm ... though one still pregnant with uncertainty.

The musical foreboding is realised with the first of the two riff-based motifs that fuse and spar on 'Part IV: Bumpy Ride'. This quixotic material, which proceeds in 2/4 with an extra beat thrown in, is written and led by Steve Howe, and has an almost cartoonish, music hall quality to it. Or "futuristic math-funk", if you prefer. The impact is not altogether comfortable and jolts the ebb and flow that the piece has maintained over the preceding 14' 37". Guitar overdubs present an element of counterpoint behind ascending blocks of synth. Suspended chords and a throbbing pulse provide a slightly slower, quieter, re-stabilised version of the "dreaming" theme first stated in dramatic instrumental terms towards the end of the Overture (1:33), and recapitulated more soberly, and then vocally, in Part III (4:43). The quieter section is a deliberate delay to the resolution that follows.

Suddenly the mood lifts and changes again. Geoff Downes' keyboard trumpet peals (a musical trope he has employed several times with Asia) and an intense wash of combined instrumental elevation announces the reappearance of the predominant 'fly from here' theme on the concluding Part V. It is a rather short reprise – almost a rush to the finish line – in which the verse jumps tempo and accompaniment (0:20) and a thick, lavish instrumental flourish (1:11–1:32) finally gives way to a fairly rapid diminuendo and the sound effect of a faint control tower announcement from the distant airfield. The piece begins and ends quietly. In its beginning is its ending, and vice versa.

Overall, 'Fly From Here' is a strong piece of music that manages to combine accessibility within a broader musical landscape that incorporates a whole raft of features, adaptations, and dynamic shifts – changing tempo more often than the actual time signature (in contrast to much material in the '70s). The album therefore goes on inviting exploration and further listening – a regular quality of Yes music at its most effective. Even so, there appears to be some difficulty in the construction of the last two sections of the piece. 'Bumpy Ride', tilting from 4/4 close to 7/8, lives up to its name rather well, and the coda in Part V could be said to lack a dominant resolution. This may be because by far the boldest statement of the central 'fly from here' melody has already been offered in Part II (the bones and sinews of the original song). It is rather difficult to work out how this can be heightened further at the conclusion without pushing the boundaries of excess. Instead, Yes understandably opt for restraint in concluding 'Fly From Here'.

However, this still leaves Part IV perched at a decidedly awkward angle. It tips the architecture of the suite rather quirkily at 19:54, but without any huge musical payback, other than the slightly predictable climbing motif that – together with a downtempo shuffle – sets the scene for a major key reprise. This nevertheless feels something of an anomaly in an otherwise very neatly constructed, thoughtfully ordered and well-delivered piece. To put it another way, in a suite that is composited rather than through-composed, sometimes the joins show. There is therefore a lack of the kind of cumulative suspense, inquisition, tension and release that provides the driving logic of many of Yes's all-time classics.

Blending old and new

In a previous era, Yes albums were shaped by the constraints of the old vinyl LP record. That meant two sides of music, each no more than around 23 minutes, to avoid the degrading of sound quality in those delicate grooves. *Fly From Here*, perhaps both consciously and unconsciously, fits that mould, as well as being adaptable to today's download generations – with an almost 24-minute piece matched by five shorter songs totalling 23:11 together.

The first of the shorter tracks is Chris Squire's 'The Man You Always Wanted Me To Be' (5:08), with supplementary keyboards from Gerard Johnson and some lyrical input from Simon Sessler. The song dates back to some 2006/7 writing sessions for a Squire solo album to follow up 1975's *Fish Out Of Water*, which was subsequently abandoned. Essentially a ballad, and less immediately reflective of the group's ethos, 'The Man You Always Wanted Me To Be' nevertheless provides an immediate contrast to 'Fly From Here'.

With Squire leading the vocal line, before being joined by Benoît David (2:00) and others, the song features some relaxed, hook-flavoured but well-balanced instrumentation from Howe, White and Downes. This is in the 1990s tradition of individual group members bringing a small vignette to the band process, and then attempting to translate it into a grander Yes mode, with greater or lesser success.

From 2:40, 'The Man You Always Wanted Me To Be' begins to pick up some obvious Yes traits, including Steve Howe's sharp, rising, memorable guitar figures (0:57, 3:58 and 4.21 onwards), a late organ swell, and Alan White using hand drums. There are also Squire trademarks in both the vocal and bass departments (0:17 and 3:24ff. for instance). The result is warmly melodic and hugely superior to the misplaced 'Aliens', performed on the 2008/9 'In the Present' tour before finally being recorded (and recovered somewhat, but not much) on the the Chris Squire and Steve Hackett album *Squackett* (2012). On the other hand, it is not as evocative as the fleeting, atmospheric Squire song 'Can You Imagine' from *Magnification,* and may strike some as one of the less convincing moments on *Fly From Here*.

With 'Life On A Film Set' (5:01), we are back firmly in Horn and Downes territory, and also with their implicit vision of what Yes might be and do after the pinnacle years of progressive rock, stemming back to the immediate post-*Drama* era. This piece is in many respects a faithful reproduction of the earlier demo, but with important tweaks here and there, and some fine studio singing from Benoît David. The scene-setting opening 50 seconds are both simple and cleverly crafted on Spanish guitar, with a haunting vocal line and an ethereal flute/recorder synth (a hint of 'Your Move').

The verse, alternating with the predictable, but determinedly executed, 'riding a tiger' chorus (accompanied by, to my ears, an over-lush synth embellishment), also has darker undertones, before a short, high, harmonised vocal bridge (2:06) segues into the remarkable third section (2:12). This opens with an urgent, rhythmic acoustic guitar (*à la* Porcupine Tree on the startling 'Last Chance to Evacuate Planet Earth'), picking up the pace for an intertwined vocal and instrumental *tour de force* ('over the beaches / into the sky').

At this point Benoît David does indeed articulate at pace in the style of *Song of Seven* era Jon Anderson – not in order to copy, but to raise the song to a new level – aided by a judicious choice of echo (production-wise), weaving synth, and swift bass runs from Squire. All this before Alan White's drums and Steve

Howe's searching electric guitar enter the fray (2:53), propelling the piece forward, with a brief resolve (4:01) – until it reaches another choral precipice (4:54) from which, this time, there can be no return. The spirit of Yes shines through this piece, even if it is, compositionally speaking, 'inherited'.

Next up are two Steve Howe offerings. The first, 'Hour of Need', utilises the full group, and has been made available in two forms. The European and North American edition of *Fly From Here* has the shorter one (3:08) featuring the core song. The Japanese 'extra' version clocks in at 6:46, and includes a 52-second instrumental introduction (rather early Asia-like), and a further 2:51 of augmented instrumentation at the end. This can be related to several ascending bars from Joaquin Rodriguez's *Concierto de Aranjuez*, and features some powerful 'orchestral' playing from the whole group, led by Howe's soaring guitar lines. However, there is little thematic connection between the song material and the instrumental material, and after the vocal finale it is almost as if the rest of the music is bolted on from a different piece. Indeed that is probably what happened, given Yes's recent ways of working. It is also most likely why it was omitted from the other CD versions.

'Hour of Need' itself, shorn of these instrumental additions, is a pleasing song with a mildly elliptical melody, introduced by Howe's mandolin guitar and Squire's richly harmonic quasi-walking bass part (0:16–0:23) and then supplemented by a nostalgic but beautifully modulated synthesiser break from Oliver Wakeman (0:56–1:05). The vocal harmonising in thirds is well executed. It shows the softer side of the band, fitting with the kind of effect created by several of the lighter songs on *The Ladder* (1999), plus 'Nine Voices (Longwalker)', which closes that album and also employs a mandolin.

Steve Howe's solo acoustic contribution is entitled 'Solitaire'. It begins with a series of slightly pleading signature notes, before introducing a fingerpicked and double-stopped theme, shifting via a brief slide into an ascending Iberian-style mode – at 10, 20 and 40 second intervals respectively. This is Howe at his most precise. A strummed and plucked bridge introduces a finely picked classical motif as the piece continues to build. A repeated and amplified three-note signature gives way to a further development that also recalls the mood of Rodriguez. A variety of aural effects are employed in the continuation, including a slow, gentle flamenco. At 2:40 the second (country style) theme is revisited, concluded, and resolved with some ringing harmonics in reprise.

On the first few hearings, 'Solitaire' has a slightly tentative feel to it. But it grows in stature, coherence and timeless authority with each new listen. Howe's ability to switch effortlessly between different styles, phrasings and effects while still producing a continuous guitar narrative is the fruit of years of practice, writing and performing. It all comes together very well here, in a piece that has a great deal more to it than initially appears to meet the ear. 'Solitaire' also distinguishes itself from other Howe acoustic solos on past Yes albums – 'Clap' (*The Yes Album*), 'Mood for a Day' (*Fragile*) and 'Masquerade' (*Union*). It does so by eschewing a dominant influence – country, classical or modern folk in those three cases – in order to build a piece of music blending a set of attributes that might initially seem ill-fitting, but which combine convincingly in the end.

Beyond the storm?

The final flourish on *Fly From Here* is produced by a driving, robust group composition, 'Into the Storm'. This has a heavier feel to it than anything else on the album, echoing *Drama* in that respect – but equally the livelier portions of *Tormato*, and 'South Side of the Sky' on *Fragile*. It also follows, intentionally or otherwise, a '90s tradition of Yes songs hinging on an aggressively abrupt main introductory theme. The other examples here are 'The Solution' (*Open Your Eyes*) 'Finally' (*The Ladder*) and 'Dreamtime' after the orchestral overture (*Magnification*). In this case the power chords rapidly give rise to a rhythmically tricky theme whereby the bass drum is in 3/4 while the rest of the kit is in 4/4. Then Steve Howe's ringing guitar announces, extends and enfolds the instrumental line. The smoothness of the vocal harmony (0:51) establishes itself in contrast to the abrasive introduction. "Something not so superficial...", declare the lyrics. It sounds a bit like a manifesto for the New Yes – or perhaps a comment on a piece of music that is in certain respects what was aspired to, but not achieved, with the *Open Your Eyes* sound-mix.

Everyone performs well on 'Into the Storm'. Downes contributes textural, highlighting synths and piano. David tackles some sinewy vocal lines (ones that also demand clarity) adroitly. But it is perhaps Squire and Howe who stand out – the former for his chunky, flanged bass, the latter (especially 4:42) for digging out another commanding, divaricating set of lead guitar lines. The pace is stepped down towards the end, as the different instruments blend more meditatively and Howe adds a few featherlite acoustic touches to steer 'Into the Storm' towards a placid musical port. Altogether, a strong concluding statement for the album.

How to assess this CD overall? Unlike some of the band's post-1994 recorded offerings, *Fly From Here* comes together cohesively as statement. The suite idea generally works well, leaning towards multilayered complexity in popular form, without merely trying to ape past accomplishments or styles. There are, inevitably, question marks. Regarding some of the keyboard patches, for example, do the reedy, retro elements really help what is otherwise a well-constructed, textural approach? Likewise, the decision to head once more into 1999-and-beyond augmented ballad territory will not necessarily please those who aspire to purity about conforming to the core grammar and syntax from the band's 'main sequence'. But that's OK. For as Chuck Klosterman says, if you claim to like everything you probably like nothing. On the other hand, that doesn't mean you have to dismiss what is not your preference. So although it will never be a favourite of mine, I am content to acknowledge that *Fly From Here* manages to draw out and gel significant strengths from the six musicians involved at a time when all might have been far from accord. The voice of each can be heard distinctly, while the band as a whole comes across univocally. That is quite an achievement after all these years and yet another line-up reconfiguration. Yes may have "lost some of their grandeur", as Ernesto Lechner once put it (perhaps a good deal of it, in the cold light of day), but the time for valedictory judgements is not quite yet.

Chapter 12
Second Attention (2012–2018 and beyond)

The more you look at the known, the more you see that there's even more unknown than you knew before.

– Steve Howe, April 2014

It was on Friday 9th December 2011 that Benoît David appeared for the last time as lead singer for Yes, at the Sporthallen in Solna, Sweden. Three final dates on the tour supporting the *Fly From Here* album (in Finland, Estonia and Russia) had to be cancelled when his voice gave out. The rest of the band – Howe, Downes, Squire and White – acted rapidly. They recruited Jon Davison, latterly singer with progressive band Glass Hammer, but also a bass and guitar player in his own right, to step up to the microphone. His first appearance was in Auckland, New Zealand, on 1st April 2012. It was no April Fool. Indeed, it went well. Davison was an accomplished vocalist whose voice was readily capable of covering the range that had, in the end, proved too much for David, and which was essential to delivering Yes music. He also had a comfortable stage presence and brought with him compositional skills that his predecessor had mostly been lacking. Not only had the band landed on its feet again at a time of potential crisis, but also they had opened a new door to the future, it seemed.

The touring continued with 12 dates in the Pacific Rim (2012), 30 dates in North America, nine in South America and then back for another 27 shows in the USA again (all in 2013). After the first dozen concerts the *Fly From Here* material was dropped in favour of packages featuring the band's better-known and more popular work during the 1970s. But it was clear that if Yes was not to become more of a heritage act, with only two new albums in the course of more than twelve years, something fresh was needed. Jon Davison set about visiting and getting to know the other members of the band, collaborating extensively on the writing of new material. The resulting album, *Heaven & Earth*, was recorded at the Neptune Studios, Los Angeles, California, from 6 January to 14 March 2014, ahead of the Spring 2014 North American and European 'three album tour' (featuring *Close to the Edge*, *Going for the One* and *The Yes Album*). It was released on 16 July that year, after the release of official snippets of material on the Internet, and the leaking of several tracks in less than optimum grade MP3s.

Heaven & Earth peaked at number 20 in the UK album chart, the band's highest position since *Talk* in 1994. It got as far as number 26 in the US Billboard 200 chart. The album was almost instantly controversial, both among fans of the band and among the critics. There was positivity from Yes aficionados towards some of the longer tracks like 'Subway Walls', 'Light of the Ages' and 'Believe Again', but a feeling from many others that the album as a whole lacked energy and pace, especially in the bass and drums/percussion department. There were well-crafted melodies and well-delivered harmonies, but some evidence that producer Roy Thomas Baker (coming back to complete his relationship with the band after the debacle of the Paris sessions at the end of the 1970s) had pushed them more into a disappearing mainstream than others would have wanted them to go. Billy Sherwood came in at the end with his proven skills to finish the mixing, having previously engineered the backing vocals. But it still felt if there was a missing ingredient, especially when (with hindsight) *Heaven & Earth* became the last Yes album to feature the towering bass figure of co-founder Chris Squire, who tragically died of acute erythroid leukemia on 27th June 2015.

Conflicting perspectives
Artistically, the title of the album created expectations of something monumental, which this particular musical process was never likely to deliver. The heaven and earth metaphor was intended to reflect, at some level, the tension and relationship between the possible and the available, the spiritually nourishing and the grounded – a regular strand running through Yes music … and perhaps an implicit, unintended question about whether a group with such an illustrious past, seemingly in search of some unfinished song or symphony, could still journey forward in a way that does justice to what had been its highest aspirations.

Visually, Roger Dean had provided a blue-hued landscape with touches of white, green and red that had an almost Japanese aesthetic feel. But the delicacy and detail amidst washes of colour and texture in the artwork did not always echo the musical pattern of the album. Squire described it as "accessible but still adventurous". However, the level of adventure was pretty mild by Yes standards. Instead, there was an aura of nostalgia about aspects of *Heaven & Earth,* with songs like 'In a World of Our Own' and 'It Was All We Knew' seemingly referencing thoughts of yesteryear, rather than the search for fresh horizons. 'To Ascend' also refers explicitly to "memories of once longer days". Yes in curatorial mode. For musicians several of whom are on the cusp of 70 years, that is of course entirely understandable. But it is not what has gained the band its reputation.

The difficulty of getting the album a more positive reception in some quarters was not made easier by aggressive 'no Anderson, no Yes' or 'no Wakeman, no Yes' keyboard warriors online, either. Nor did it help that the band was willing only to use three of the new songs on tour, 'The Game' in 2014 and 'Believe Again' in 2014 and 2015, in the USA, Australia and Japan (but not in Europe). 'To Ascend' was presented at just six concerts. Equally, as with *Fly From Here*, the heavily song-oriented slant of the album lost it recognition among some of those committed to the longer, more adventurous Yes works of the '70s. After the initial flush of publicity, individual band members also started to go colder on *Heaven & Earth*, with Steve Howe in particular regretting the rush that had been required at the end of recording and post-production. The material, he seemed to suggest, had just not been given the space, time, development and appropriate kind of collaborative culture required to make it Yes music of a higher calibre. All of this means that, in this case as in many others, it is challenging to listen without prejudice, but always rewarding to try.

An album of contrasts
Heaven & Earth begins with a kind of personal testimony from vocalist Jon Davison, who wrote the majority of lyrics for the album, with the obvious exception of Howe's 'It Was All We Knew'. The opening track, 'Believe Again', is about what is involved in recovering a sense of hope that you fear you have lost. It is rich melodically, welding a number of ideas together and featuring a filigree repeated Moog figure in the middle that undoubtedly harks back to another Yes era, without fully going there. The song went down well in concert. At 8' 02" it perhaps outstays its welcome a little upon repeated listens, but it is nonetheless an effective and inviting opener. Its pace is more stately than exuberant, introduced and thoughtfully punctu-

ated by Steve Howe's steel guitar.

Interestingly, 'The Game', another well-designed ballad featuring ideas from Gerard Johnson and Chris Squire in sessions from some years earlier, is also introduced by steel guitar and features attractive bridge phrasing from Howe. It is a song of experience: "We all know the rules, the game / Us fools, still we play the same / As if our days remain." What counts is what we do, not simply what we say, and "the love we gave along the way." There is something almost valedictory about this lyric. Once again, Davison's vocals are foregrounded, and the melodies he creates are curvy and pleasing. They become more memorable over time. This remains one of my favourite tracks on the album.

By contrast, 'Step Beyond' is a song that I could happily leave behind, with its cloying surface and nagging synth wiggle. Equally, I am not sure that 'In a World of Our Own', which for some reason recalls for me Jon Anderson's 'Don't Forget (Nostagia)', from *Song of Seven* (1980), when he was trying to reclaim his roots post-Yes, is especially beneficial to the case for *Heaven & Earth*. The problem with both is not so much that they are popular in style. So is 'It'll Be a Good Day' from *The Ladder*, and that is much more successful. The difficulty is that they lack the distinctiveness and emotional resonance involved in the best Yes music that is of a not-especially-progressive kind.

In between these two songs, we also have the charming ballad 'To Ascend', which contains definite echoes of early Anderson-influenced Yes. The instrumentation is delicate and perhaps a fraction too sweet for my taste. The acoustic version (sticking with acoustic guitar and keys for accompaniment, and available on the Japanese release of the album) conveys this appealing little song particularly well.

The last three tracks on the album are, along with the first two, among the strongest. Matters of musical reminiscence are very subjective, of course, but 'Light of the Ages' conjures up for me the feeling of Genesis in their *Wind and Wuthering* era. The instrumental introduction features bell-like keys, variation of dynamics on drums and bass, and a teasing lead line on steel guitar. The verse and chorus of the song have a folky texture, with strummed acoustic and steel highlights. The bridge from 2:54 to 4:07 showcases some neat ensemble playing and harmonising before moving back to the main vocal theme. The core impact of the song comes from the exchange of affirmative and more questioning motifs, lyrically and musically. Is what troubles us the dominant reality, or will life and light win through? In the final analysis, it is possible that "I'll heed the primal sound / Exposing the grand scheme / I can see it's a dream / Sorrow's a dream." At 7' 41", 'Light of the Ages' seems to offer rather more to the listener than the slightly longer 'Believe Again', and might be one of several Yes pieces that could benefit from further development through concert rendition. It is one that advocates of *Heaven & Earth* certainly want to hear performed live.

'It Was All We Knew' acts almost as a palate cleanser between this worthy song and the extensive and telling final track on the album. Full of shimmering summer sun, it begins with a beckoning instrumental lick before dissolving (0:30) into a breezy vocal reflection on 'the windy road of misadventure', giving way to a sense of unity beyond it all. In younger days, of course, "Sweet were the fruits / Long were the summer days / It was all we knew". Here is an older, wiser commentator looking back with some gratitude, but not without a sense of life's struggles and human frailty. This song, written by Steve Howe, could almost have come off his 1993 solo album, *The Grand Scheme of Things*, which is indeed referenced lyrically on *Heaven & Earth*. It also features a delightful slice of bright, almost skittish, guitar work. Maybe not everyone's idea of Yes, but a smile-inducing little gem for me.

The last word on this curiously diverse album is 'Subway Walls'. Here we are most obviously on progressive rock terrain again – a territory really only hinted at earlier. But the value of this track is surely not to be found in our ability to fit it into some prog mould, but in the quality and expansiveness of the playing. In online conversation around the time of the album's release, Geoff Downes remarked that his keyboards were "all over this". And he is right. The opening synth instrumental is lushly orchestral, with tuned percussion (from 00:49) and a sudden diminuendo into the Hammond-led segue (1:30) towards a bass and guitar figure that prepares for the song. A more urgent drum and bass call introduces Davison's angularly scanned opening declamation (2:13). The shifting tempo gives way to an elevated, lingering choral statement (2:42–3:07) of the main lyrical question: "Is there meaning in the stars / Or does graffiti on some subway wall / Hold the secrets to it all?" Are there, indeed, any secrets to be mined at all, we might ask, or do we mostly read meaning into the available signage?

Jon Davison's determination to live life in the positive lane appears a little more hard-won than Jon Anderson's sweeping gnosticism these days. A second vocal theme ("The victory of game / It's all a state of mind", 3:09–3:39) leads back to a restatement of the previous one, then onto a fresh bass riff joined by drums and organ (4:40). Downes' fine Hammond solo is followed by an equally uplifting one from Howe (5:22–6:15). The vocals return for a final statement: "Oh, wounded sparrow of my heart / Your time has come / So soon will you mend." Then we are into a really powerful coda (6:59–9:05) – "Brave the battle that's before you / Transcend." This grandeur, carried on a falling and rising cascade of notes from Steve Howe, is how Yes really should sound, many will feel. It is full of passion and intensity, resolved in a long organ chord filled out with bass pedals and a lighter synth line. Here is a worthy *dénouement* to an album whose promise exceeds its realisation, and which leaves us with the tantalising question of what on earth might follow next…

Before and beyond

The virtue of the otherwise uneven *Heaven & Earth* is that it is clean and clear in its presentation, arrangement, articulation and production. Its weakness is that, in many respects, it is neither fish nor fowl, neither one thing nor another, musically speaking. It has a rich sound palette, but obviously lacks pace and energy. It offers tasters of different Yes possibilities, but no clear direction. It contains echoes of the band from an earlier era, but is much less certain about where the creative impulse of the group lies now. Despite some riches (for me the best tracks are 'Subway Walls', 'The Game' and 'Light of the Ages'), Yes feels too comfortable and lacking in the fruits of real creative tension on this album. Nick Reed's review for *The Quietus* (2nd July 2014) captures, in his personal summation, the ambiguity lurking in every corner:

> It may be an easy album to tear down, but truthfully, I kind of like some of these songs.

Maybe the truth is that *Heaven & Earth* came a little too late as far as Chris Squire was concerned, and a little too early in terms of Jon Davison's developing role and the arrival of Billy Sherwood on bass after Squire's sad demise. For Sherwood has undoubtedly added fresh energy, commitment and impulse to the current band, in spite of the huge loss of a defining member.

Touring from 2015–2017, and preparing for fiftieth anniversary surprises in 2018, Yes certainly feels like a group more at home in its own skin than it has been for a number of years. Personal relations appear cordial. There is a warmth that has sometimes been absent. Revisiting *Drama* and *Tales From Topographic Oceans* has proved a good move, highlighting two eras in Yes's history where they were at their most musically assertive. The ego level has also come down considerably, as can be seen in comparison to the Anderson Rabin Wakeman (ARW) project and the tensions evident during Yes's overdue but decidedly uncomfortable induction into the Rock'n'Roll Hall of Fame on 7th April 2017.

The band now seem more approachable than ever for many of their fans, but the question of what they do next artistically, and how they either wrap things up or pass the flame onwards after fifty years, is a large one. Will Yes take their next decisions purposefully, or will what transpires happen to them in a more circumstance-driven way? Will 'Yes featuring ARW', whose contribution so far has been live renditions of earlier material (see the next Chapter) make a serious legacy claim with an album of original material in 2018 or 2019? With this band – or with either, as we might be forced to say – it is generally impossible to predict. If there is to be a summation of the twisting, varied plot that has been Yes music, it deserves to be a strong one. At present the gap between what has been in recent years, and what was back in the day, is large. The rhetoric may be overblown, but just consider this paean of praise from Dan Hedges in the 1974 American Winter tour programme and wonder:

> Today [the band's publicist wrote some 44 years ago], Yes are acclaimed throughout the world. They stand apart from trends and fashions. They rise above the ordinary plains of pop. They are acknowledged as artists not only by millions of fans ... but also by serious musicians and critics whose sympathies are usually reserved for more traditional or conventional modes of music.

He continues:

> Yes have evolved from writing simple 32 bar songs to creating complete, complex works that are not symphonies, or operas or oratorios or anything else the world has ever known. What they produce has no recognizable name for their work is utterly new. Their work is truly the result of group activity rather than the child of a single dazzling mind. The whole group is a

single dazzling mind. Instruments and voices are employed as an orchestra and choir, weaving a tapestry of sound that is overwhelming in its final impact. Their music must be appreciated as a whole rather than as a series of pieces that may be contemplated in isolation.

Might this be how Yes music could be seen in another fifty years? If so, how could what happens in 2018 and beyond possibly relate to that kind of legacy? To ground that question, we cannot but note that *Heaven & Earth* is, at the time of writing, the last album Yes has produced. Whatever worthy hints it contains concerning what their music has been or still can be, it quite clearly does not merit being a final statement. Whether such a statement in album form will be (or should be) forthcoming at this juncture is, in Steve Howe's paradoxical words, "even more unknown than you knew before." Most long-term listeners are probably doubtful. But rule nothing out in the topsy-turvy world of Yes.

Chapter 13
Passions That Flow
(*Yes live*)

Music is a performance and needs the audience.

— Michael Tippett, composer

It has often been observed that Yes playing live is a very different proposition for many people than Yes on disc or via download. That is true of all music at some level, of course – but perhaps especially so for the kind of music that has a strong and inescapable element of visual spectacle, space and theatre about it. Critics who suggest that Yes can sometimes sound technical, clinical and lacking in warmth on their studio albums may therefore be taken aback when hearing them afresh in concert. I know I was.

For me, listening to the band live for the first time during the *Going for the One* tour at the Empire Pool, Wembley, on 28th October 1977 – coincidentally the Feast of St Simon and St Jude – was a life-changing musical experience. The sheer power, depth, range, structural beauty and subtlety of 'Close to the Edge' and 'Awaken' took my breath away. According to Derek Jewell (writing in 1980 in *The Popular Voice: A Musical Record of the 60s and 70s*), jazz legends Johnnie Dankworth and Cleo Laine were also there, soaking in a very different musical atmosphere to their usual haunts like Ronnie Scott's. At that stage in the band's life, Yes music crossed many boundaries and brought together people from quite different backgrounds. That is a key part of what made it what it is.

As Jewell also noted in *The Sunday Times* on 30th October 1977:

> [Yes] couple the driving excitement of rock with all those reflective, lyrical, imaginative and virtuosic blessings which come from other kinds and qualities of music.

That sums it up very well. This is music for the head, the body and the human spirit all together. For those who have fallen under the spell of the Yes muse, what the band offer at their finest are inimitable moments where the power of rock, the spaciousness of classical music and the daring of jazz or world music combine and spark something quite new and unexpected. Equally, for their many detractors, such a fusion proves unstable, overwrought, irritating, incomprehensible or unnecessary. Each, in the last analysis, to their own.

Touched by sound

Where the music of Yes finally comes together or falls apart, and either proves or betrays itself, however, is in the live concert. For it is here that the notes leap off the recorded artefact or page and come to life, animated by an audience, projected into the ether, and falling upon the ears of the listener in a series of singular, unrepeatable moments. Sure, there are live recordings – unofficial ones galore, and a number of official releases of varying quality. But none of these really capture 'the live experience'. I can vividly recall, for instance being in the front row and more-or-less dead centre for an intimate (by Yes standards) night at the House of Blues in Orlando on 22nd October 1999, during *The Ladder* tour. At this proximity you get monitor sound as well as a close up view of the musicians. I can only describe it as like being embraced in a wall of music – at once clear as well as loud, dynamic as well spacious, detailed as well as grand. For those few hours it felt as if you were in a sound bubble, shared with a fortunate few, in which the music you knew so well was transfigured and transported to a different level ... without, I should add, any chemical assistance!

Other standout tours where the spine tingled and the heart leaped included 'Masterworks' in 2000, when the Anderson / Howe / Squire / White / Khoroshev line-up delivered the finest versions of material from *Close to the Edge*, *Tales From Topographic Oceans* and *Relayer* that I have ever heard first-hand. In its own way, the 1991 *Union* tour (on which I attended all five UK concerts) was also a highlight. Listening back to recordings of 'Awaken' from those evenings I am not unaware of how over-the-top the eight-piece Yes arena band was; but there is something crazily magnificent in there, too. The same thought might apply to the 2001 *Symphonic* tour, which again projected long-form Yes music with cinematic and orchestrally enhanced range, intricacy and conviction.

These concerts are imprinted in an un-erasable way on my mind and soul. So, surprisingly for me, is the *Talk* tour. The 1994 show at Jones Beach was especially energising, illustrating how the '80s-derived west-coast version of Yes could employ an arena to convey the majesty of Yes music, even with songs that were, by comparison to the early- to mid-'70s, stripped back and simplified. More recently, hearing Billy Sherwood step into the bass role for the first time after the tragic death of Chris Squire in 2015 was also a special musical moment. Like Jon Davison in the vocal department, Sherwood is his own man. But he also deeply inhabits the band's music and the spirit of those who have produced it (not least the mercurial Squire), and is able both to transmit it on its own terms and bring to it something 'other', with his Telecaster-shaped red Carvin bass in place of Squire's classic, heavily modified Rickenbacker 4001.

There are also the gigs that got away, of course. Inexplicably, despite having started really to appreciate the music of Yes by then, I declined a chance to hear the band at Queens Park Rangers in 1975. That turned out to be a legendary concert, captured imperfectly in video form on *Yes: Live – 1975 at QPR* (1993). Not seeing the band in '75 and missing out on some sparkling 'in the round' performances in 1978, due to the illness of a close friend, ranks for me among other unrecoverable missed live opportunities – like not seeing Frank Zappa, turning down a ticket for what turned out to be Miles Davis' last concert in the UK, being too ill to go to The Smiths' last ever gig in Brixton, and missing composer Michael Tippett's final London concert appearance before his death, due to public transport travails.

It is what you miss out on, as well as what you gratefully hear, that reinforces just how special a live concert will always be. So do those in-concert 'misses', of course. Many of us have experienced frustrating occasions when someone has felt impelled to yell out or chatter during a quiet acoustic passage, or to impose their frame all over the sightline on the assumption that their need to dance badly is more important than others' need to see. Then there are the unavoidable flaws occasionally coming from the stage. Trevor Horn's failing voice in England in 1980 is a painful memory, especially given how important *Drama* proved to be with musical hindsight. Likewise, Benoît David's vocal struggles on some nights, and the 2014 tour where Chris Squire was fading and the performances fell short of the unreasonable standards Yes has set in the past. Poor quality YouTube videos have proved especially unhelpful (and unrepresentative) at these and difficult, contested moments of Yes's concert career. There are lapses we cannot overlook, for sure. But they do not need to become destructively definitional. With Tony Kaye (keys) and Jay Schellen (drums) joining the band on stage for the 2018 'Cruise to the Edge', Yes has now performed live as a five-piece, a six-piece, a seven-piece and an eight-piece band over the years.

Live recordings

Among the official recorded artefacts that are available, *Yessongs* (Atlantic, 1973) is widely regarded as a classic, even though the technology was primitive, acoustic moments are compromised, and as someone once said (Dan Hedges, I recall), the sound quality is such that it feels like the band is checking in from a phone box. Digital re-mastering has worked wonders here and elsewhere, nonetheless. *Yes Years* (1991) contains a live recording of the band in its prog pomp incongruously covering The Beatles 'I'm Down' as an encore from Roosevelt Stadium on 17th June 1976, with a surprise guest appearance by Led Zeppelin guitarist Jimmy Page. Meanwhile, *Progeny: Seven Shows from Seventy-Two* (Rhino, 2015) is a fine comparative account of the band in that formative era, and it is to be hoped that other classic concerts from 1974 to 1978 might be forthcoming in this series, as well as 'Masterworks' in full. *Yesshows* (Atlantic, 1977) also offers outstanding performances of 'The Gates of Delirium' and 'Ritual'.

Another highlight, both on CD and DVD, is *Live at Montreux 2003* (Eagle, 2007), which features an entrancing version of 'Awaken'. The *Symphonic* CDs and DVDs, recorded in the Netherlands, are also a strong document of the 2001 tour, with everyone on good form and Tom Brislin excelling on keyboards. *House of Yes* (Eagle, 2000) is likewise powerful, and *Union Live* (Voiceprint, 2011) has its moments, along with *The Word is Live* (Rhino, 2005) and *ABWH* concert material. Steven Sodebergh's *9012Live* movie (1985), shot at Northlands Coliseum in Edmonton, Canada on 28th and 29th September 1984, is a distinct moment in rock videography in its own right, alongside the *9012Live: The Solos* album. Additionally, *The Word is Live* contains various curios: an early Yes cover ('It's Love', the Young Rascals) and 'For Everyone', part of which eventually became 'Starship Trooper'. Also featured is a concert rendition of the unrecorded *Drama* era song, 'Go Through This', featuring some quirky rockabilly guitar from Steve Howe.

All that said, in my view there is nothing so far, either by way of official sound or video recording, that has quite succeeded in showing Yes at their very best in concert. But there are moments on most of the available releases (see Appendix I: Discography) that give more than appreciable hints. The re-released early material, such as *Something's Coming: The BBC Recordings* (New Millennium, 1997) is definitely worth checking out.

Last but not least, at the other end of their career, the latest *Topographic Drama: Live Across America* release (Rhino, 2017) sounds good and gives a positive account of the current band, albeit lacking on disc the energy that can be felt palpably in the concert hall. It will also be interesting to see what 'Yes featuring Anderson, Rabin and Wakeman' offer by way of the glorious contradiction that is, as Robert Fripp would no doubt sternly remind us, the 'live recording' – a fractured digital space in which at least something of the past can become both present and future.

Finally: music beyond words

For each listener, every live experience of Yes will be different, naturally. Post-concert reviews, both amateur and professional, soon confirm that. Yet there are also moments of shared human emotion, illumination and understanding to be gained. For in listening to Yes in concert over the years, what can be discovered, I would suggest, is that while rock music can indeed be gauche, brash, "dried up by fads" and prone to "hideous failings in taste and judgement" (American writer Greil Marcus), so it can also produce "moments of unbelievable clarity and invention, pleasure, fun ... excess, novelty and utter [energy]".

Before I offer some tentative thoughts on Yes in a wider musical context and the legacy of the band in the next two Chapters, I need to sound a necessary warning about what has preceded and what will follow. While this and other voluminous writings on the band (see Appendices II and IV) hopefully offer some different gateways into the music, they are no substitute – merely signposts that will or will not connect and indicate, according to time, interpretation and circumstance. The 'live experience', which is, at the end of the day, integral to music, makes the point with abundant, ceaselessly renewable clarity. Michael Tippett puts it well in *Music of the Angels* (Ernst Eulenburg, 1980), when considering the mysterious, abstract 'condition of music' to which, Walter Pater famously suggested in his 1873 essay on Giorgione, all art ultimately aspires.

Tippett declares:

There is knowledge concerning [music], and this knowledge is something quite different from the immediate apprehension of works of [music], even from whatever insight we feel we have gained by perceiving and responding to works of [music]. A simple statement such as: [music] must be *about* something, is innocent enough till we want to give a name to this something. Then invariably we delude ourselves with words, because ... we cross over into the field of writing or talking *about* [music]. We have reversed ourselves.

We have indeed, and the only antidote is to allow the music to speak on its own inimitable terms once more. To 'go live' again.

Chapter 14
Yes After 'Progressive Rock' (50 years and onwards)

> To study music, we must learn the rules. To create music, we must break them.
> — Nadia Boulanger

> There are two kinds of music. Good music, and the other kind.
> — Duke Ellington

> Progressive rock is anything that doesn't sound like regular rock. Regular rock is everything that sounds like itself.
> — Frank Zappa (MTV interview, 1984)

> Whither progressive rock music? I would much prefer to let that old fashioned terminology fall back into the swamp of its indulgent insignificance.
> — Peter Banks (in his memoire, 2001)

Ah, the dreaded bunny-ears around the term 'progressive rock'. Those quotation marks indicate the fearful truth that we are about to get into something of a friendly dispute about terms; in this case the one that is most regularly applied to Yes and the music the band have produced over 50 years, to pigeon-hole it, praise it and dismiss it. For better or worse, Yes are seen as among the originators and pioneers of 'prog' as an (alleged) musical genre, as the publicity for this book unavoidably reminds us. I would prefer to think about it the other way round. If the best of their work is dubbed 'progressive', then progressive rock, whatever that might be, clearly has something to be proud of. But if the label puts people off, we have a problem. As I suspect we do.

We cannot live without labels and boxes of course. We need somewhere to place the goods we cherish, including music, in order to understand, relate to and communicate them. But, by the same token, those handles and hold-alls can become a barrier to appreciation and understanding. "Look in the light of what you're searching for." So sang Jon Anderson on Yes's nu-disco simulacrum, appropriately entitled 'Dangerous', on the often-reviled *Union* album (1991). He had a point. Inverting that a little, what we seek often exists in a shadow fabricated by the tools of apprehension with which we have chosen to investigate. When our major tool is a hammer, we are likely to see every issue or problem as a nail, it has been said. And so it is with music. Set up a definition of 'progressive' rock (or one of its synonyms), stare hard into the distance, and you will discover, most likely, something fitting the mould of your preconceptions. Then you can laud it, praise it or discard it. In fact you might just end up doing all three. For those lines stretching outwith the window you look through can turn out not to be horizons beyond, but horizontal prison bars.

Against 'symphonic rock' and other critical traps

This imprisoning of Yes's music has happened on so many occasions, and with parallel typologies. Take 'symphonic rock' for example. Though often merely used as a way of saying 'orchestrated', the term most meaningfully implies drawing on a tradition of long, complex writing in something akin to sonata form, which is simply not what Yes (or bands operating in the same general space) have done – though Rick Wakeman has talked about his use of 'classical principles' in certain songs, such as 'And You and I'. John Covach,[*] even as he identifies parallels with bits of classical composition in Yes music, acknowledges that his is a figurative rather than prescriptive analysis. In different ways, Edward Macan and, especially, Thomas Mosbø (*Yes: But What Does It Mean?*) undertake extensive 'classical treatments' of Yes music, with Mosbø particularly seeking to surface sonata form in *Tales From Topographic Oceans,* and other Yes work, in some considerable detail. This enterprise is most definitely not without interest.

In the end, however, we have to acknowledge that orchestral textures, collaborations and quotations in Yes music are just that: features, rather than premeditated structural elements, or signs of an overwhelmingly intentional approach to composition and arrangement in a consciously classical vein. So the terminology of 'symphonic' or 'orchestral' rock easily creates expectations and assumptions (as well as, for some, fears) that the music cannot and does not need to meet, and which may obscure a more helpfully direct appropriation of said music as a distinct hybrid form founded on the shores of rock but capable of responding to waves and inspirations from other sources.

By way of example, the CD entitled *Symphonic Music of Yes* (RCA Victor, 1993), which features input from Jon Anderson, Bill Bruford and Steve Howe, alongside the London Philharmonic Orchestra, the English Chamber Orchestra and the London Community Gospel Choir, is to me a disappointing affair, despite a brave attempt at orchestration by David Palmer. It ends up sounding thin, gimmicky and uncomfortably like

---

[*] See 'Progressive Rock, "Close to the Edge", and the Boundaries of Style', in John Covach and Graeme M. Boone (eds.), *Understanding Rock: Essays in Musical Analysis.*

a *Muzak* Yes in places. By contrast *Yes: Symphonic Live* (Eagle Entertainment 2010), though still not actually 'symphonic', is a fine DVD and CD recording of a Netherlands concert on the 2001 tour, featuring the European Festival Orchestra. The arrangements are really effective, allowing the orchestral instruments to supplement and enhance the live band, without pretending that this is somehow a classical fusion or representative of music that comes from another tradition.

There are also genuine 'orchestral style' moments on several Yes albums, of course. Snatches of *Relayer*, for example, or the opening of 'Subway Walls' (*Heaven & Earth*). But these work because they stand out from the flow, not because they are normative. As Steve Howe has said, what Yes does is, above and before all else, founded in rock music. Add the adjectives and qualifiers to that, by all means, but do not try to ignore the manifest or press it into the service of some other cause or ideology. Equally, of course, rock music now includes Yes, whatever some critics may wish. This means the vocabulary of rock can and should be stretched, expanded, challenged and complemented. That is all to the good. It is what a live artistic tradition should be all about.

Terms of endearment?
It is surely better, then, to keep our terms of reference, categories and typologies as flexible, modest and open as possible when it comes to this kind of music. Not least to forestall a totalising approach. In proposing, cheekily, that, "there are two kinds of music. Good music, and the other kind," Duke Ellington was precisely arguing against the illegitimate use of musical categories to accept or reject wholesale, or to assign value *en masse* to a particular type of music but not to another. He was thinking about jazz, sneered upon by self-appointed musical elites. This 'category dismissal' is often what has happened with the term 'progressive rock', too, and not just with Yes. The label has been used as a cipher to rule things in or out, to pronounce

something sound or unsound. It has invited some to pay attention in once place, when their attention might best have been deployed elsewhere; and it has effectively stopped some pundits from listening with any care at all. They have thereby become cultural arbiters of 'acceptable' taste, rather than music critics or signposters.

That, of course, is as much about people as labels. When someone says, "I hate prog rock", or "I hate classical music" or "I hate jazz", or "I hate soul", they are generalising from one particular experience, taking these terms to be some kind of catch-all, or simply letting you know that they haven't listened very far at all. I would once have said, I'm sure, "I hate country music." Then someone looked at me and said, "Really? You've listened to all of it, have you?" I laughed. And then I was introduced by my wonderful wife (who has no interest at all in Yes) to the sublime song-craft of Laura Cantrell, upon hearing which I *almost* said, "But that's not my idea of country music" ... and then I got it. The problem was exactly "my idea" and confusing it with the enormously variegated set of traditions that country music in fact embraces, from Johnny Cash (his dark, final album is an extraordinary statement) to things that are, well, nothing at all like Johnny Cash.

Why do people despise 'prog'?
It is the same, unsurprisingly, with 'prog'. When people claim they hate it, and you ask them what they hate, it often turns out to be "endless twiddling solos" or "pretentious lyrics", or "pointlessly complex time signatures" or "preposterous stage shows", or "empty virtuosity". Now all these things can, of course, be found in the denizens of what is readily labelled as progressive rock. Then again, they can be found in other musical territories and genres too (such as glam rock and metal, which often attracts acceptance from those more readily dismissive of prog). Incidentally, I dislike most of those traits in overabundance too, but I am less convinced, through listening

and observation, that they apply to Yes at their best, or to all of Yes – just as I am pretty sure that not all of Yes's music can be usefully labelled 'prog', and that whether it is or not is no basis upon which to value or disvalue it.

So is there any way out of this definitional pickle, and does it matter? The way forward (if not 'out', that may be too much to ask) is, I would suggest, both to reshape and to loosen our terms of reference sufficiently to allow the actual music to breathe. Doing this matters in so far as the categories we currently employ (consciously or otherwise) may be inhibiting both our capacity to appreciate particular musical experiences and our ability to approach, comprehend and respond to new things in music. It matters quite a lot, in other words.

A good fresh starting point, I think, is Frank Zappa's observation, made in an interview recorded for posterity on Talk-Classical.com – one that clearly flummoxed his original MTV interviewer back in 1984. Progressive rock, he suggested, is rock music that doesn't just go on sounding like itself, following the same conventions, sticking to industry formula, trying to please a shifting market without regard to artistic aspiration or endeavour. Zappa continued:

> All songs that sound the same. Everything on MTV. Everything on the radio. That's 'rock.' Progressive rock is stuff that doesn't sound like that.

Absolutely, I would say. For while 'progress' can be a dubious category (a teleological belief that things must somehow always be moving towards a 'destination', developing with a view to a previously hailed 'improved' or more 'advanced' condition), what we can be absolutely sure of is that commodification is the death of creativity and innovation in music. Therefore *creativity* is perhaps the least contentious way of talking about 'progress' in musical terms. It means openness to fresh ideas, new perspectives, transgressed boundaries, varied horizons and different languages. It means rejecting financial reward or popularity as final arbiters of taste, value and the relationship between the two. It may even mean a non-naïve return (a *ressourcement*) to musical spaces of inspiration where, in a different time or context, such possibilities were deeply treasured – like Yes in the era of *Close to the Edge*, *Tales From Topographic Oceans* and *Relayer*, I would argue.

However, trying to copy or ossify a particular musical style or vocabulary from that (or any) specific era is by definition not 'progressive' at all, but profoundly regressive. It is stuckism writ large, whatever you try to call it. Too much that passes for progressive rock these days (and reading through the excellent *Prog* magazine, I'd be the first to acknowledge that there are many musicians in that orbit who do not want to be stuckists at all) can easily slip into that mistake. In Yes circles they are likely to be found among the "No Jon [Anderson], No Yes" brigade, or those who judge everything since 1972 against the iconic album from that year, or those who recognise no value to the songs that do not readily conform to a 'prog' style they prefer, or those whose listening is restricted to the mainstream defined by a commercial industry. None of that is 'progressive' (by which I mean, as I have said, fuelled by the instinct to be creative). It's not wrong, of course. It is a preference. It is just one that is not going to get the music very far.

From 'progress' to open creativity in music

Zappa's definition of rock that could meaningfully be called progressive is, then, one based on resistance to all formulas that first squeeze music through a process of consumer validation on consumption terms. Are Yes progressive, he was asked? Are King Crimson, are Genesis? "Sometimes", was his consistent, honest and (in my view) correct answer. Of his own output he observed:

> I wouldn't describe myself as progressive rock either. In fact a lot of the time it's not rock and roll at all, it just happens to be [listened to] by rock and roll audiences.

Indeed, Frank was unafraid to stretch rock into vaudeville, to turn its harmonic language inside out, to veer into deformed jazz and twisted contemporary classical music. He was a pioneer, a re-skiller, an impresario, a collaborator, a transgressor, a violator of norms, and a technical and compositional auteur. That's creativity, whether you call it progressive or rock or anything else. I'd probably prefer to call it 'out rock', 'rock-based fusion', or 'post-rock' (though that latter term has already been claimed, so maybe, more humorously, 'après-rock').

In their stimulating book, *Beyond and Before: Progressive Rock Since the 1960s* (2011), Paul Hegarty and Martin Halliwell say:

> One of the best ways to define progressive rock is that it is a heterogeneous and troublesome genre – a formulation that becomes clear the moment we leave behind characterizations based only on the most visible bands of the early to mid-1970s.

The difficulty, they and others point out, is that prog's scope is often limited to a series of aforementioned stereotypes about long solos, concept albums, fantasy lyrics, grandiose stage sets and costumes, along with an allegedly obsessive dedication to technical skill. This, in turn, is pinned on sets of bands and writers associated with a particular era (who may or may not exhibit those tendencies). But the reality is inevitably more complex. What gets called progressive rock is inherently varied and founded on fusions of styles, approaches and genres, tapping into broader cultural resonances that link to avant garde art, classical and folk music, jazz, theatrical performance and moving image, without necessarily purposely emulating, absorbing or continuously referencing any of those forms most of the time. In addition, the label 'progressive' is likely to require or imply more poetic lyrics, technology being harnessed to generate new

Chapter 14 Yes After 'Progressive Rock' • 191

sounds, music approaching a condition that could be called 'art', the importation of wider harmonic language into the rock sphere, a concern with music for listening rather than dancing, and a general willingness to defy standard pop or rock formulae and expectations.

In these terms, those of a creative drive capable of resisting commercial pressure, the music of Yes could be described as progressive "sometimes", but by no means all the time. For chunks of their musical career, the band has been content to import elements of creative music and performance into a more standard rock or stadium context. Some of the music that has come out of these attempts (often conditioned by the pressures of lack of resources and control, as Bill Bruford has pointed out) is to my taste, some is a little less so. The quality, energy and spirit of Yes has nevertheless more than survived most of its incarnations, I would contend. But its most abiding value is shaped by, and emanates from, some of their earlier work – especially in the period 1971 to 1977, with bursts of energy and flashes of inspiration throughout the '80s, '90s, '00s and beyond.

In Appendix III: Yes Classics, I have attempted to give shape to this contention by identifying what I regard as the most abiding and high quality music they have produced across all 21 studio albums to date. What, in other words, I think might last as a testimony to, and abiding legacy of, the unparalleled creativity the band unleashed from its early years and 'classic' period across its whole body of work. I am, of course, bound to be wrong about this. In terms of what will be remembered in 50 years time, well beyond my lifetime – these could well be some of the classics: *The Yes Album*, *Fragile* and *Close to the Edge*, for sure, together with *Going for the One*, *Drama*, *90125* and possibly (to the surprise of some) *Talk*, along with songs and fragments from elsewhere. I sincerely hope that it will also include recognition and rehabilitation for *Tales* and *Relayer*, because in my estimation those, along with *Edge*, are the most boundary-pushing musical creations Yes ever did or will produce. That is why the Chapters about them in this book are by far the longest. Equally, whatever the definitional, commercial or musical fate of 'progressive rock', I believe Yes music deserves recognition and attention well beyond its 50th anniversary in 2018. That will only happen if more people are prepared to let go of the labels and assumptions that prevent a creative listening, which is, in turn, a listening for the creative and the inspiring in many musical genres. In those terms, Yes music can indeed survive, and, hopefully, thrive.

Yes tomorrow: in the future is the beginning?
It is, of course, unclear how far the existence and development of either of the two current iterations of Yes, the official band and the one featuring Anderson, Rabin and Wakeman (established early in 2016), will contribute to the long term custody and appreciation of the music in which they have all played an important part in generating and preserving to date. Back in 1991, Rick Wakeman said that he believed it possible that in a hundred years time there could still be a Yes out there. Perhaps, he and others have mused, the band could turn out to be something like an ongoing, developing ensemble of creative musicians, carrying on the spirit and tradition of the band, and above all its music. Ironically, Wakeman has gone on bitterly to resent the coming of a new voice and different keyboard players to the group he evidently is still hugely attached to, just as he failed to connect to two of the albums, *Tales* and *Relayer,* which many would regard as absolutely critical to any present or future Yes canon. Equally, however, he may turn out to be right in his later rather than earlier belief – essentially that Yes is a creature of its time, tied to certain traditions embodied in the musicians who have passed through it, and destined to disappear when those resources are finally exhausted. Better to go out in a blaze of glory than fade into insignificance, others would say. That is not for me to judge. I will be content if I have merely helped

Chapter 14 Yes After 'Progressive Rock' • 193

someone (anyone) listen to, appreciate, revisit or reconsider any of the music of Yes, or if something in these pages has simply helped enhance the pleasure and value of such listening.

As to the context in which Yes music will or should be listened to after 50 years. Well that, too, is a necessarily moving feast. I have noted original guitarist Peter Banks' trenchant disregard for the term 'progressive rock' (back to those quotation marks again). It is a disregard that Robert Fripp would share in more studied and deliberative form in relation to the appropriate context for hearing King Crimson, too. Steven Wilson (Porcupine Tree and beyond) has been similarly questioning. The 'prog' label, many would say, is simply too poisoned by expectation, dismissal and lazy stereotyping. It is also trapped by the inadvertent acceptance of the terms of rejection of the music so categorised by some of those who most wish to affirm it – the charge perhaps a little ungenerously thrown at authors Bill Martin and Edward Macan by Hegarty and Halliwell. Others might wish to mount a case for the defence, or, in my case, advocate a switch of terminology (to something like 'out rock' or 'rock-based fusion') in order to invite questions rather than formulaic responses. In any event, it remains a persistent curiosity that the output of the band considered in this book is constantly referred to, by followers and critics alike, as "Yes music". That is something of an acknowledgement – advertent and inadvertent in different contexts – that the music produced by Yes has for many listeners an indefinable feel and aura to it (perhaps especially during the 'classic' era of the 1970s) that stands out from any attempt to label it definitively.

In summary, creativity in music today is increasingly less patient with the boundaries established by collectors, critics and curators, and that has to be a good thing. Those most able to follow in the tradition of Yes will therefore not be seeking to copy its forms and procedures at all, but will be responding artistically to its spirit in their own context and with their own energy. For if 'progressive' means anything in musical terms, and in terms of rock music specifically, it is about an approach, not a sub-genre. It signifies a certain willingness to give priority to artistic creativity and, at some level, to innovation. In those terms some of Yes's music fits the bill and some does not. But the important thing, in the final analysis, is whether it moves your heart, your soul, your head ... your whole: yes indeed – viva music!

Chapter 15
Coda: Total Yes Retain?

We were convinced that you could make music that was in the underground tradition, but you could do it and present it in a way that was available for everyone to enjoy.

– Rick Wakeman

Time flies, on and on it goes
Through the setting sun
Carry round and round...
Until it comes to carry you home.

– Yes, 'Future Times / Rejoice'

So, as the central question in 'The Revealing Science of God' (1973) puts it ... what happened to this song we once knew so well?

Back in those dim, distant 1970s, Yes helped define what people saw as a new musical genre, combining sounds and textures from a variety of sources to produce – by rock standards – lengthy, elliptical compositions. In the 1980s they began to restyle themselves for a very different era, achieving their greatest commercial success in the process. Since then they have travelled back and forth, through many highs and lows, seemingly in search of some mislaid song or symphony that has continued to elude while never failing to entice.

Many, of course, would argue that the (apparently) lost chord was found and was played only for it to abandon them. But, failing to 'feel the sound' in the right way, the band still continued to experiment and reformat forlornly. In so doing Yes merely ended up repeating or losing itself over the next 40 or so years, reaching not a fitting *dénouement* but a pale imitation of itself embodied in two groups of musicians dedicated above all to preserving the past. So the story goes for some followers and detractors of Yes, perhaps especially those schooled and locked in the 1970s.

But there is another way to look at things. It is possible that, taking into account the whole musical panorama the band has laid out – which, I have argued, cannot in fact be appreciated adequately within the limiting prism of 'progressive rock' – there is a valid sense in which it possible, simultaneously, to fuse two elements in listening ever more attentively to the music of Yes. The first involves holding out for a defining era, a canon, or a series of illuminating moments that amount to a 'mountain top experience'. The other entails recognising that there is differential value across the whole 50 years of Yes history, and beyond. You do not have to choose one stance over the other. That is not how it works. Both can be true. As I have absorbed and been absorbed by Yes music over the years, I have discovered, I believe, a sense in which, to adapt the title of the second phase/mini-movement of 'Close to the Edge', it is possible that the total mass of the band's music can indeed be retained, even as some of it is foregrounded and other parts of it slip from memory or attention at different stages of our appreciation.

Arguably, of course, while recognising that each era of the band's output has its merits, it might be necessary to say that 'Close to the Edge' or 'Awaken' were still the musical peaks that could never be scaled again. Or maybe it was 'The Gates of Delirium', or one of the four sides stretching out over the monumental *Tales From Topographic Oceans*? Certainly, as I have

Chapter 15 Coda: Total Yes Retain?

discovered in writing *Solid Mental Grace*, those are the places where the lion's share of my attention has gone. Those who love Yes music, and those who have loved it and left it, all have their own view of what that elusive, definitive Yes 'moment in time' is, or was. Most would agree that it never quite came round again, and probably never will in a creative, innovative sense.

But that may not matter in the broader scheme of things. For the song that almost sang itself out on 'The Revealing Science of God', only to emerge on 'Ritual', before making fleeting appearances on albums and at concerts ever since, is not something that can be captured, commodified or contained. It is as it is, and then it passes, leaving its own distinctive trail of longing, emotion and aspiration imprinted on the listener. Anyone who has fallen for the Yes muse will have some idea as to what that means. For others it may remain a distraction, a diversion, or perhaps a mystery best left to its own devices. So be it.

The conundrum enshrined in those alternating positive, negative and disinterested instincts towards the music of Yes is, like the song or the symphony that truly evokes something of importance, never likely to reach a conclusion upon which all can agree. Certainly not in this book, possibly not ever. Consensus is not the point; inspiration is – something that can be felt and evoked, but never quite experienced second hand, let alone bottled and passed on for instant profit.

Intellectually, I am tempted to agree with Bill Bruford. It was probably always the case that Yes could never have gone beyond (or back to) the musical heights they scaled in the early 1970s, not least the one in which Bruford was himself involved before leaving the group, the magisterial album *Close to the Edge*. So would it not have been better for the band to rest things there and find new musical pastures, fresh challenges as their original drummer/percussionist did? As composer Philip Glass once observed:

> If you don't know what to do anymore, there's actually a chance of doing something new.

There's a strong case to be made for that. And yet ... as we have seen, there was and is more – much more – to be discovered by those who have travelled on with the band through the dark, light and sometimes grey years ahead – and those re-discovering the band.

For example, while it may not be comparable to 'And You and I', the musical landscape of Yes would be poorer, I would suggest, without 'I'm Running' from *Big Generator*, a song of considerable invention, flexibility and daring. So it is with countless other pieces of music outside what is often regarded as the main sequence of Yes music up to 1977, including – for example – 'On the Silent Wings of Freedom', 'Machine Messiah', 'Hearts', 'Miracle of Life', 'Endless Dream', 'Mind Drive', 'That, That Is', 'Fortune Seller', 'New Language', 'Spirit of Survival', 'Into the Storm' and 'Subway Walls'. These offerings (or others that could have been selected from all the post-1978 albums, plus whatever emerges musically from the band in 2018 and beyond) may be viewed by some as flawed gems compared to others of undeniably abiding value. But they are all, in their own way, occasions of joy, anticipation, thoughtfulness, subtlety, power and realisation – which is what, ultimately, that heady concoction we call Yes music provides.

My own musical frontiers have stretched well beyond and before Yes, of course. I would be rather worried if they hadn't. Sometimes, talking to those attending the band's more recent gigs, I *am* worried! The musical culture revolving around a certain style of 'mainstreamed' progressive rock can be very limiting, as original guitarist Peter Banks argues at the end of his often trenchant memoir, written with Billy James, *Beyond and Before: The formative years of Yes*. But at the passing light of easing, on this particular textual journey in sound, I realise that there will never be a place in my heart that is closed to the

Chapter 15 Coda: Total Yes Retain? • 199

music of Yes; or that does not need it as part of a rich, changing and varied diet of sound. At the end of the day that kind of realisation lies way beyond any analysing. For we either are, or are not, "caught within the spell".

That is what music is all about. Yes, oui, si…

> One thing learned from all these years
> As stupid now as we were at first
> Maybe that's the way it goes
> When you try to change the world
>
> – 'Into the Storm', 2011

Acknowledgements

This is always the most perilous part of completing any publishing project, since the fear of leaving out people who you later really wish you had included is considerable, and the debt owed to many, in the grand scheme of things, is great. The usual caveat about those named here bearing no responsibility for the failings or oversights herein naturally applies.

First thanks go to my wonderful publishers, Bob Carling and Maria C. McCarthy. I'm delighted to be stabled with Cultured Llama, and it is a pleasure to work with them. I am especially grateful to Jonathan Crawford (http://www.jonathancrawford.com) for his fine cover image, friendship and support, and to my brother-in-law, Kevin Roth, for the unique photograph of Chris Squire from 1978. Huge thanks also to Carla J. Roth for putting up with this part of my life over 22 plus years, with little advance warning. I love you.

Much of what I know of things Yes is owed to two people: Henry Potts, in whose house I was a lodger when I lived nearer to London, and whose attention to detail on 'Yes – Where Are They Now' and in other musical and scientific contexts is legendary. Also to Steven Sullivan of Forgotten Yesterdays, Yesgigs 1968–1980 and New York fame. Both were denizens of the infamous Alt.Music.Yes around the same time as me.

Over the years I have made a good many fond friends and acquaintances through Yes concerts, tours and events. Author David Watkinson and Scottish network galvaniser Brian Neeson deserve a special mention, not least for the incredible work they have been putting into the band's fiftieth anniversary celebration at the end of the 2018 UK tour and beyond, and for including me in the roster. Jon Kirkman was supportive when I corresponded with him in the early days of this project. Thomas Mosbø and Carol Fay Mosbø are wonderful people. Other folk I've established good musical vibes with and want to acknowledge include Ash Armstrong (see you at the opera one day!), Ruth Zurawka and Jim Tauberg, Alison and Brian Lancaster, John Connor, Krista Wallhagen (wishing you health and happiness), Mark Rasicci, Rhea Frankel, Roy DeRousse, Dave Fagan, Ian Parry, Ian Weatherhill, Eriko Kurokawa, Steve Chappell, Paula Jakobi, Anne Corris, Joe Cass, Pam Bay, Jamison Smeltz, Miguel Falcão, Charles Imperatori, Tiz Hay, Donald Hay, Lizzie Blundell, Malcolm McLean, John Kuehne, David Westbay, Richard Adam, Mark Watterson, John Kuehne, Dave Owen, Jean Neeson and Simon Bourne – plus any I've inexcusably forgotten due to my increasing years. Also in memory of Andrew Wakefield, Merry Celeste, and Malcolm Birkett, plus with warm wishes to Scotty and Xilian Squire.

Then there are those people whose paths I cross in other spheres of life, but who I discover I have some kind of Yes connection with, sometimes to my great surprise. They include David McLachlan, Ruth Gouldbourne, Anne Rhiannon Richards, Stuart Roberts, John Eje Thelin, Alastair Murray, Alistair McBay, David Denniston, Paul Goodwin, the remarkable Rachel Mann (thank you so much for the Foreword), Neill Walker, Paul Martin, Jamie Pitts (the first two albums), plus Rob Levick and Tom Hurcombe. Neither should I forget those who have resourced me musically in other ways in recent times, way beyond the orbit of this book: Jordan and Shona Tchilingirian, Steve Lawson, Pat Bennett, Mark Fisher, Ian Dommett, Gerry Hassan, Simon Jaquet, Stephen Plaice, Marcia Bellamy, Jill Segger, Alistair Thorn, Fiona McTaggart, Morag Balfour and many more. Their special role is to feel delightfully free of any responsibility whatsoever for what precedes.

The brief extracts from Yes lyrics that I have quoted, strictly for purposes of review, analysis and comment, are used with full acknowledgement and thanks to the copyright holders in each case – in particular Topographic Music Limited, Island Music Limited, Affirmative Music (BMI), MCA Inc., Beyond Music and Soul Food Music. In their assigned form, these may be found online. My final 'thank you' is evidently to all in and associated with Yes who have, over the years, created the music which is the delight, critical focus and interest of this book. They have, of course, no responsibility for the views and contentions of the author.

About the Author

Simon Barrow is a writer, critic, journalist, commentator, educator and researcher. Based in Edinburgh, Scotland, he is known for his work in the fields of politics, beliefs and ethics. Music (ranging from Early Music and Baroque through to contemporary classical, art rock, experimental soundscapes, electronica and jazz) has been a constant companion in his life. Simon is director of the public policy think-tank Ekklesia and has contributed to a wide range of print and digital publications. He has also followed the ebb and flow of progressive rock band Yes for approaching 45 years, and has seen the group and its individual members in concert on more than 100 occasions across four countries and two continents during that time. Though he has published on culture and music for a number of print publications over the years, and wrote regularly for the blog NewFrontEars from 2002 to 2008 (with a few forays since then), *Solid Mental Grace: Listening to the music of Yes* is his first book in this area. Initially conceived ten years ago, it appears now to coincide with the band's remarkable fiftieth anniversary. Simon Barrow is also a long-term advocate of the music of the English composer Michael Tippett, and is currently planning and writing a book in appreciation of Tippett's music, life and artistic vision.

More material connected with this book can be found on the web: YesSolidMentalGrace.com, on Facebook: www.facebook.com/solidmentalgrace/ and on Twitter: @YesSolidMentalGrace.

Appendix I: Discography

The recordings listed here, and referred to throughout the book, relate to original UK releases. Dates and companies may vary with US, Japanese and other releases. The asterisked albums are not official Yes releases, but ABWH ones. Yes featuring Anderson, Rabin and Wakeman have not released an album at the time of publication of this book (March 2018).

In terms of studio CDs, the Rhino Remasters Series (with bonus tracks) and the Steven Wilson 5.1 remixes of earlier Yes albums are recommended. These can be found readily through online suppliers. Only official live releases and concert videos are included here, plus a selection of compilation albums and some select solo work from Yes *alumni*.

Yes Studio Albums
Yes (Atlantic Records, 1969)
Time and a Word (Atlantic Records, 1970)
The Yes Album (Atlantic Records, 1971)
Fragile (Atlantic Records, 1971)
Close to the Edge (Atlantic Records, 1972)
Tales from Topographic Oceans (Atlantic Records, 1973)
Relayer (Atlantic Records, 1974)
Going for the One (Atlantic Records, 1977)
Tormato (Atlantic Records, 1978)
Drama (Atlantic Records, 1980)
90125 (Atco, 1983)
Big Generator (Atco, 1987)
Anderson, Bruford, Wakeman, Howe (Arista, 1989) *
Union (Arista, 1991)
Talk (Victory Music, 1994)

Keys to Ascension (Essential, 1996)
Keys to Ascension 2 (Essential, 1997)
Open Your Eyes (Eagle Records, 1997)
The Ladder (Eagle Records, 1999)
Magnification (Eagle Records, 2001)
Fly From Here (Frontiers, 2011, plus a limited edition remix with Horn on vocals, *Fly From Here – Return Trip,* 2018)
Heaven & Earth (Frontiers, 2014)

Live Yes Albums

Yessongs (Atlantic, 1973)
Yesshows (Atlantic, 1977)
9012Live: The Solos (Atco, 1985)
An Evening of Yes Music Plus: ABWH (Caroline, 1994)*
Something's Coming: The BBC Recordings (New Millennium, 1997)
House of Yes: Live from the House of Blues (Eagle Records, 2000)
Symphonic Live (Eagle Rock, 2002)
The Word is Live (Rhino, 2005)
Live at Montreux 2003 (Eagle, 2007)
Live at the NEC: ABWH (Gonzo Multimedia, 2010)*
Union Live (Voiceprint, 2011)
In the Present: Live from Lyon (Frontiers, 2011)
Songs from Tsongas (Image Entertainment, 2005/ 2014)
Like It Is: Yes at the Bristol Hippodrome (Frontiers, 2014)
Progeny: Seven Shows from Seventy-Two (Rhino, 2015)
Like It Is: Yes at the Mesa Arts Center (Frontiers, 2015)
Topographic Drama: Live Across America (Rhino, 2017)

Select Compilation Albums

Yesterdays (Atlantic Records, 1975)
Classic Yes (Atlantic Records, 1981)
Yesyears (Atco, 1991)
Yesstory (Atco, 1992)
Symphonic Music of Yes (RCA Victor, 1993)
Affirmative: The Yes Solo Family Album (Connoisseur Collection, 1993)

Highlights: The Very Best of Yes (Atlantic, 1993)
Yes, Friends and Relatives (Eagle, 1998)
Yes, Friends and Relatives, Vol 2 (Eagle, 2000)
Keystudio (Sanctuary, 2001)
In a Word: Yes (1969–) (Rhino, 2002 / 2008)
The Ultimate Yes: 35th Anniversary Collection (Rhino, 2003)
Yes Remixes (Rhino, 2003)
Essentially Yes (Eagle, 2006)
The Studio Albums 1969–1987 (Rhino, 2013)

Videos of Yes in Concert and in the Studio
Yessongs (1975)
9012Live (1985)
YesYears (1991)
Greatest Video Hits (1991)
Yes: Live - 1975 at QPR (1993)
Live in Philadelphia (1995)
Keys to Ascension (1996)
House of Yes: Live from House of Blues (2000)
Symphonic Live (2002)
Yesspeak (2004)
Yes Acoustic (2004)
Songs from Tsongas (2005)
Live at Montreux 2003 (2007)
Classic Artists: Yes (2007)
Yesspeak Live: The Director's Cut (2008)
The Lost Broadcasts (2009)
Rock of the '70s (2009)
Union Live (2011)
In the Present – Live from Lyon (2001)
Live Hemel Hempstead Pavilion, 3 October 1971 (2014)
Like It Is: Yes at the Bristol Hippodrome (2014)
Like It Is: Yes at the Mesa Arts Center (2015)

Selected Solo and Collaboration Albums from Yes *Alumni*

Jon Anderson: *Olias of Sunhillow* (1975), *Song of Seven* (1980), *Animation* (1982), *Three Ships* (1985), *In the City of Angels* (1988), *Deseo* (1994), *Change We Must* (1994), *Angels Embrace* (1995), *Toltec* (1996), *Lost Tapes of Opio* (1996), *The Promise Ring* (1997), *Earth Mother Earth* (1997), *The More You Know* (1998), *Survival and Other Stories* (2011) and *Open* (2011). Also significant collaborations with Vangelis, Rick Wakeman and others – most recently 'Invention of Knowledge' (2016), with Roine Stolt.

Peter Banks: *Two Sides of Peter Banks* (1973), *Instinct* (1994), *Self-Contained* (1995), *Reduction* (1997) – all re-mastered and reissued as a set in 2018. *Can I Play You Something?* (The Pre-Yes Years Recordings From 1964 to 1968, 1999). *Trying* (with Harmony in Diversity, 2006). Work with Flash, Empire and The Syn.

Tom Brislin: *Hurry Up and Smell the Roses* (2012), plus his work with Spiraling, Camel, The Syn and others. Tom is also a keyboard tutor and writer.

Bill Bruford: *Feels Good to Me* (1978), *One of a Kind* (1979), *Gradually Going Tornado* (1980), *Music for Piano and Drums* (with Patrick Moraz, 1983), *Flags* (with Patrick Moraz, 1985), *If Summer Had Its Ghosts* (with Ralph Towner and Eddie Gomez, 1997), *Live at the Jazz Café* (with ProjecKcts, 1997), *Bruford Levin Upper Extremities* (1998), *Every Step a Dance, Every Word a Song* (with Michiel Borstlap, 2004), *In Two Minds* (with Michiel Borstlap, 2007), *Skin and Wire, The Music of Colin Riley* (with PianoCircus, 2009), and all his work with King Crimson and with Earthworks – which cannot be recommended highly enough.

Benoît David: his work with Mystery, including *Beneath the Veil of Winter's Face* (2007), *One Among the Living* (2010), *The World is a Game* (2012) and *Tales from the Netherlands* (2014).

Jon Davison: his work with Glass Hammer, including *If* (2010), *Cor Cordium* (2011), *Perilous* (2012), *The Inconsolable Secret* (2013 re-recording) and *Ode to Echo* (2014). With Sky Cries Mary, *Taking The Stage: 1997–2005* (2011).

Geoff Downes: *The Light Program* (1987), *Vox Humana* (1992), *Evolution* (1996), *The World Service* (2000), *Shadows and Reflections* (2003) and *Electronica* (New Dance Orchestra, ft. Anne-Marie Helder, 2010). With Buggles, *The Age of Plastic* (1980), *Adventures in Modern Recording* (1981). With Chris Braide, *Skyscraper Souls* (2017).

Steve Howe: *Beginnings* (1975), *The Steve Howe Album* (1979), *Turbulence* (1991), *The Grand Scheme of Things* (1993), *Masterpiece Guitars* (with Martin Taylor, 1996), *Quantum Guitar* (1998), *Portraits of Bob Dylan* (1999), *Natural Timbre* (2001), *Skyline* (2002), *Elements* (2003), *Spectrum* (2005), *Motif* (2008), *Time* (2011). Plus the *Homebrew* series of demos and many collaborations, most recently *Nexus* (with Virgil Howe, 2017). See also the Steve Howe Trio,

The Haunted Melody (2008) and *Travelling* (2010). Plus, on DVD, *Steve Howe's Remedy Live* (2005).

Tony Kaye: *The End of Innocence* (2012, online). *Flash* (with Flash, 1972), *One Live Badger* (with Badger, 1973), *Circa* (with Circa, 2007), *Yoso* (with Yoso, 2009), *Live in Japan* (with Billy Sherwood, 2016), *Valley of the Windmill* (with Circa, 2016) and others. Circa and Yoso are Yes spin-off bands that have also involved Alan White and Billy Sherwood. With Sherwood and others: Mabel Greer's Toyshop, *New Way of Life* (2014), featuring material by Squire.

Igor Khoroshev: *Piano Works* (1999), *Encores, Legends, and Paradox, A Tribute to the Music of ELP* (appearance, 1999), the soundtrack to *Good Night Valentino* (2003).

Trevor Horn: a host of production credits, plus, with Art of Noise, *Who's Afraid of the Art of Noise?* (1984), *The Seduction of Claude Debussy* (1999), *Reduction* (2000) and *Reconstructed* (2004). With Buggles, *The Age of Plastic* (1980), *Adventures in Modern Recording* (1981). US/The Producers/The Trevor Horn Band, *Made in Basing Street* (2012).

Patrick Moraz: *The Story of i* (1976), *Out in the Sun* (1977), *Future Memories Live on TV* (1979), *Les Musiques de la Première* (1987), *Windows of Time* (1994), *PM in Princeton* (1995), *Resonance* (2000), *ESP* (2003), *Change of Space* (2009), *Live at Abbey Road* (2012; live recording from 1987). Plus *Music For Piano and Drums* (with Bill Bruford, 1983), *Flags* (with Bill Bruford, 1985), *Music for Piano and Drums: Live in Maryland* (2012; live recording from 1984, with Bill Bruford). Many film soundtracks and other projects. Also: 'Three Dances for Two Prepared Pianos' on *A Chance Operation – The John Cage Tribute* (1993).

Trevor Rabin: a number of solo albums, especially *Can't Look Away* (1989) and *Jacaranda* (2012), plus numerous soundtracks scored for major movies.

Billy Sherwood: *The Big Peace* (1999), *No Comment* (2003), *At the Speed of Life* (2008), *Oneirology* (2010), *What Was the Question?* (2011), *The Art of Survival* (2012), *Divided by One* (2014), *Citizen* (with Chris Squire's last recorded bass on the title track, 2105). Also many collaborations, *World Trade* (1989) with World Trade, plus Conspiracy and Circa albums.

Chris Squire: *Fish Out of Water* (1975) – limited edition re-master with extras issued by Cherry Red Records in 2018, *Conspiracy* (with Billy Sherwood, 2000), *The Unknown* (with Billy Sherwood, 2003), *Chris Squire's Swiss Choir* (2007), *Squackett* (with Steve Hackett, 2012) and a variety of sessions and collaborations. With Esquire, 'To the Rescue' (1987). With Mabel Greer's Toyshop, *Images* (2016, re-mastered recordings from 1967–1968). With The Syn, *Original Syn* (2004/5), *Indestructible* (2005). Some live recordings are available of The Chris Squire Experiment, which segued into Conspiracy. Last track recorded: 'Citizen' (Billy Sherwood, 2015).

Oliver Wakeman: *The Three Ages of Magick* (with Steve Howe, 2001).

Rick Wakeman: well over 100 solo albums and many collaborations, the best of which are probably *The Six Wives of Henry VII* (1973), *Journey to the Centre of the Earth* (1974), *Criminal Record* (1977), *At Lincoln Cathedral* (2005) and *Piano Portraits* (2017). Sessions with David Bowie (*Space Oddity*, 1969; *Hunky Dory*, 1971), Cat Stevens ('Morning Has Broken', 1971) and Lou Reed (*Lou Reed*, 1972, with Steve Howe), among many others.

Alan White: *Ramshackled* (1975), *White* (2006) and *Levin Torn White* (2011), plus his legendary session work with John Lennon (Imagine, 1971) and with George Harrison (*All Things Must Pass*, 1970). See also *Live Peace in Toronto* (1969).

Appendix II: Bibliography

While this is not a comprehensive reading list on Yes, progressive rock, the experience of listening and related musics, the one hundred plus titles here should provide a very substantial set of resources for following up clues in this book about the band and its catalogue. I have listed all the key books that have been published in English (mostly), French, German, Hungarian, Italian, Japanese, Portuguese and Turkish about the band, plus some key selected chapters about Yes in other books. There is material in Czech and Dutch to be hunted out as well. The transcriptions listed and noted in book form are ones that I have collected or referred to since 1975. All authors/titles and dates in the main text refer back here.

For those starting out listening to the music of Yes and wanting the narrative context, Chris Welch's band biography, Tim Morse's collection of quotations, the fine but limited-edition interview collections by Jon Kirkman, David Watkinson's visually-oriented take and Bill Martin's not uncontroversial treatise are good places to start. Welch and Kirkman, in particular, know the band well over the years and have been professionally engaged with them. Dan Hedges wrote the first 'official biography' (up to 1980), and Martin Popoff is the latest re-teller of the tale. A number of books about the band are self-published and of varying quality. All but a few of the titles listed here are within my own library at the time of writing. There is, of course, a mass of material on Yes in magazines and journals published over the years, quite a bit of which can be tracked down online for those with the inclination. See also Appendix IV: Further Resources.

About Yes and its musicians
Cem Akkilic, Ahment Asaf, *Yes* (Studyo Imge, Turkey, 1997).

Appendix II: Bibliography • 209

Paolo Battigelli and Armando Gallo, *Yes* (Fratelli Gallo, Rome, Italy, 1985).

Peter Banks with Billy James, *Beyond and Before: The Formative Years of Yes* (Golden Treasure Publishing, 2001).

Bill Bruford, *The Autobiography: Yes, King Crimson, Earthworks and More*, (Jawbone Press, London, UK, 2009; revised edition, Foruli Classics, London, UK, 2013).

Stuart Chambers, *Yes: An Endless Dream of '70s, '80s And '90s Rock Music* (General Store Publishing House, Burnstown, USA, 2002).

Pete Clark, 'Yes: Tales of Mysticism and Imagination', in Ashley Brown (ed.), *The Marshall Cavendish Illustrated History of Popular Music – Volume 15* (Marshall Cavendish, New York, NY, USA, 1990).

John Covach, 'Progressive Rock, "Close to the Edge", and the Boundaries of Style', in Covach and Graeme M. Boone (eds.), *Understanding Rock: Essays in Musical Analysis* (Oxford University Press, New York, NY, USA, 1997).

Lionel Daloz, *Yes, Un Sentiment Océanique dans le Rock* (Editions Eä, France, 2009).

Roger Dean with Martyn Dean, Colin Greenland and David Lucas, *Magnetic Storm* (Dragons World, Limpsfield, UK, 1984).

Roger Dean with Carla Capalbo, Donald Lehmkuhl and Dominy Hamilton, *Views* (Dragons Dream Ltd, Limpsfield, UK, 1975).

Brian Draper, *Yes in Australia* (Double Bay, NSW, Australia, 2010).

Jordi Sierra i Fabra, *Rick Wakeman: Myths and Legends of the Yes Wizard* (Música de Nuestro Tiempo, Spain, 1977).

Alan Farley, *The Extraordinary World Of Yes* (iUniverse, Lincoln, USA, 2004).

Garry Freeman, *Yes – A Live Guide 1968–1979* (Helter Skelter Publishing, forthcoming).

Decio Fsngarnisa, *Yes: Uma Raca Musica de Quiriteto* (private publication, Brazil, 1999).

Gary P. Hampson and Mark Edwards, 'Awaken: The transformative lyrics and music of the progressive rock group, Yes' (via Academia.edu, accessed 6 January 2018).

Dan Hedges, *Yes: The Authorized Biography* (Sidgwick and Jackson, London, UK, 1981).

Randall Holm, '"Pulling Back the Darkness": Starbound with Jon Anderson', in Michael J. Gilmour (ed.), *Call Me the Seeker: Listening to Religion in Popular Music* (Continuum, New York, NY, USA, 2005).

Dirk von der Horst, 'Precarious Pleasures: Situating "Close to the Edge" in Conflicting Male Desires', in Kevin Holm-Hudson (ed.), *Progressive Rock Reconsidered* (Routledge, New York, NY, USA, 2002).

Steve Howe with Tony Bacon and Miki Slingsby, *The Steve Howe Guitar Collection* (Balafon Books, London, UK, 1994).

Jon Kirkman, *Time and a Word: The Yes Interviews* (Stereo33Books, 2015). Limited-edition, folio quality hardback and artwork version. An Easy on the Eye Books 175-page paperback edition is due on 28 May 2018.

Jon Kirkman, *Yes/Dialogue* (Stereo33Books, 2017). Limited-edition, folio quality paperback.

Shiloh Koluda, *Yes* (Ongaku Tomo, Tokyo, Japan, 1979).

Aymeric Leroy, *Yes* (Éditions Le mot et le reste, Marseilles, France, 2017).

Jaime Lopez, *Yes* (private publication, Spain, 2000).

Bill Martin, *Music of Yes: Structure and Vision in Progressive Rock* (La Salle, Open Court, Chicago, USA, 1996).

Tim Morse, *Yesstories: Yes in Their Own Words* (St Martin's Griffin Publishing, New York, NY, USA, 1996).

Thomas Mosbø, *Yes: But What Does It Mean?* (Wyndstar, Milton, WI, USA, 1994).

John R. Palmer, 'Yes, "Awaken", and the Progressive Rock Style', in *Popular Music*, volume 20, pp. 243–261 (Cambridge University Press, Cambridge, UK, May 2001).

Martin Popoff, *Time and a Word: The Yes Story* (Soundcheck Books LLP, London, UK, 2016).

Scott Robinson, *Yes Tales: An Unauthorized Biography Of Rock's Most Cosmic Band in Limerick Form* (Writers Club Press, iUniverse Inc., Lincoln, USA, 2002).

Will Romano, *Close to the Edge: How Yes's Masterpiece Defined Prog Rock* (Backbeat Books, Milwaukee, WI, USA, 2017).

Michael Rudolf, *Yessongs: Round About Jutesack* (Wehrhahn Verlag, Hannover, Germany, 2001).

Scott D. O'Reilly, *Yes and Philosophy: The Spiritual and Philosophical Dimensions of Yes Music* (self-published, 2012).

Jennifer Rycenga, 'Tales of Change Within the Sound: Form, Lyrics and Philosophy Within the Music of Yes', in Kevin Holm-Hudson (ed.), *Progressive Rock Reconsidered* (Routledge, New York, NY, USA, 2002).

Tomas Vasvary-Toth, *Yes: The System of Rock* (PCD Multimedia Kfd., Hungary).

Rick Wakeman with Martin Roach, *Grumpy Old Rock Star and Other Wondrous Stories* (Preface Publishing, London, 2008).

Rick Wakeman, *Say Yes! An Autobiography* (Hodder & Stoughton, London, 1995).

Appendix II: Bibliography

David Watkinson, *Yes: Perpetual Change* (Plexus Publishing, UK, 2001). Foreword by Rick Wakeman.

David Watkinson, *Jon Anderson and The Warriors – The Road to Yes* (forthcoming, 2018/19).

Chris Welch, *Close To the Edge – The Story Of Yes* (Omnibus Press, 1999, rev. 2003 and 2008, hardback and paperback).

Chris Welch, trans. Stefano Pogelli, *Fragile: La Storia Degli Yes* (Stampa Alternativa, Rome, Italy, 2009).

Dan Wooding, *Rick Wakeman: The Caped Crusader* (Granada Books, St Albans, UK, 1979).

Music transcriptions

Mick Barker (transcription) and Steve Howe (notes), *Steve Howe Guitar Pieces* (Wise Publications / Warner Bros, Secaucus, NJ, USA, 1976, reissued by International Music Publications, USA, 1999).

Mike Mettler, *Yes: Back from the Edge* (Guitar School 3, no. 5, September 1991).

Rick Wakeman with Jeff Muston, *Journey to the Centre of the Earth* (Rondor Music, London, UK, 1976).

Yes with Kenn Chipkinn and Alex Houten, *Selections from YesYears* (Warner Bros. Publications Inc., Secaucus, NJ, USA, 1993).

Yes and Carole Cuellar, *Yes Complete: Deluxe Edition* (Alfred Publishing Company and Warner Bros. Publications Inc., Secaucus, NJ, USA, 1999).

Yes and John Curtin, *Union* (Warner Bros. Publications Inc., Secaucus, NJ, USA, 1991).

Yes, *Best of Yes for Bass* (Hal Leonard Corporation, Milwaukee, WI, USA, 2013).

Yes, *Big Generator* (Affirmative Music BMI and Warner Bros. Publications Inc., Secaucus, NJ, USA, 1988).

Yes, *Close to the Edge* (Amsco Music Publishing, New York, NY, USA, 1970). Issued with 7" interview single.

Yes, *Fragile* (Charles Hansen Music & Books, London, UK, 1972).

Yes, *Fragile/The Yes Album* (Warner Bros. Publications Inc., Secaucus, NJ, USA, 1972).

Yes, *The Best of Yes* (Warner Bros. Publications Inc., Secaucus, NJ, USA, 1980).

Yes, *The New Best of Yes* (Warner Bros. Publications Inc., Secaucus, NJ, USA, 1995).

Yes, *Relayer* (Topographic Music and Warner Bros. Publications Inc., Secaucus, NJ, USA, 1975).

Yes, *Superstar Series*, volumes on bass, drums and guitar (Warner Bros. Publications Inc., Secaucus, NJ, USA, 1990).

Yes, *Time and a Word* (Amsco Music Publishing, New York, NY, USA, 1970).

Yes, *Yes/Solo* (Warner Bros. Publications Inc., Secaucus, NJ, USA, 1977).

Yes, *Talk* (Warner Bros. Publications Inc., Secaucus, NJ, USA, 1994).

Yes, *Yessongs* (Wise Publications/Music Sales Ltd., London, UK, 1973).

Yes, *Yesterdays* (Warner Bros. Publications Inc., Secaucus, NJ, USA, 1975).

Further recommended related reading about music, listening, and progressive rock

Leonard Bernstein, *The Unanswered Question: Six Talks at Harvard* (Harvard University Press, Cambridge, MA, USA, 1976).

Ashley Brown (ed.), *The Marshall Cavendish Illustrated History of Popular Music – Volume 15* (Marshall Cavendish, New York, NY, USA, 1990).

Bill Bruford, *When in Doubt Roll!* (Foruli Publications, London, UK, 1988).

Bill Bruford, 'Making it Work: Creative Music Performance and the Western Kit Drummer', doctoral dissertation (University of Surrey, UK, 2016). Available at http://epubs.surrey.ac.uk/810288/

Bill Bruford: *Uncharted: Creativity and the Expert Drummer* (University of Michigan Press, Ann Arbor, MI, USA, 2018).

Bill Bruford, 'Learning Experiences of Expert Western Drummers: A Cultural Psychology Perspective' in Z. Moir, B. Powell, G. D. Smith (eds.) *Bloomsbury Handbook of Popular Music Education: Perspectives and Practices* (Bloomsbury, London, UK, 2018).

Robert G. H. Burns, *Experiencing Progressive Rock: A Listener's Companion* (Rowman & Littlefield Publishers, Lanham, MD, USA, 2018).

Nicholas Cook, *Music: A Very Short Introduction* (Oxford University Press, Oxford, UK, 2000).

Peter Cook, *The Music of Business: Business Excellence Fused with Music* (Cultured Llama Publishing, Sittingbourne, UK, 2015).

Aaron Copland, *What to Listen For in Music* (Mentor / Penguin Books, New York, NY, USA, 1953).

John Covach, Graeme M. Boone (eds.), *Understanding Rock: Essays in Musical Analysis* (Oxford University Press, New York, NY, USA, 1997).

Macdonald Critchley and R. A. Henson, *Music and the Brain: Studies in the Neurology of Music* (William Heinemann Medical Books Ltd., London, UK, 1977 reprinted 1980). Foreword by Michael Tippett.

Appendix II: Bibliography • 213

Jerry Ewing, *Wondrous Stories: A Journey Through the Landscape of Progressive Rock* (Flood Gallery Publishing, London, UK, 2017).

Markus Freytag, *The Progressive Rock Encyclopaedia* (CreateSpace Independent Publishing Platform, USA, 2015) – essentially a lift from Wikipedia.

Michael J. Gilmour (ed.), *Call Me the Seeker: Listening to Religion in Popular Music* (Continuum, New York, NY, USA, 2005).

Paul Hegarty, Martin Halliwell, *Beyond and Before: Progressive Rock Since the 1960s* (Continuum, New York, NY, 2011).

Jonathan Harvey, *Music and Inspiration* (Faber and Faber, London, UK, 1999).

Kevin Holm-Hudson (ed.), *Progressive Rock Reconsidered* (Routledge, New York, NY, USA, 2002).

Derek Jewell, *The Popular Voice: A Musical Record of the 60s and 70s* (Andre Deutsch, London, UK, 1980).

Jon Kirkman, *Tales From the Rock Vaults* (forthcoming, 2018).

Peter Kivy, *Music Alone: Philosophical Reflections on the Purely Musical Experience* (Cornell University, New York, NY, USA, 1990).

Rich Lackowski, *On the Beaten Path: Progressive Rock* (Alfred Publishing, Los Angeles, CA, USA, 2009).

Stephen Lambe, *Citizens of Hope and Glory: The Story of Progressive Rock* (Amberley Publishing, Stroud, UK, 2011).

Daniel J. Levitin, *This Is Your Brain On Music: Understanding a Human Obsession* (Atlantic Books, London, UK, 2008).

Ian Macdonald, *Revolution in the Head: The Beatles' Records and The Sixties* (Fourth Estate, London, revised edition 1997).

Edward Macan, *Rocking the Classics: English Progressive Rock and the Counterculture* (Oxford University Press, Oxford, UK, 1997).

Bill Martin, *Avant Rock: Experimental Music from the Beatles to Bjork* (Open Court Publishing, Peru, IL, USA, 2002).

Bill Martin, *Listening to the Future: The Time of Progressive Rock 1968–1978* (1998).

John Powell, *How Music Works: A Listener's Guide to Harmony, Keys, Broken Chords, Perfect Pitch and the Secrets of a Good Tune* (Penguin Classics, London, UK, 2010).

Mark Powell, *Prophets and Sages: An Illustrated Guide to Underground and Progressive Rock 1967–1975* (Cherry Red Books, London, UK, 2010).

Anil Prasad, *Innerviews: Extraordinary Conversations with Extraordinary Musicians* (Abstract Logix Book, Cary, NC, USA, 2010). Includes interviews with Jon Anderson and Bill Bruford.

Cesare Rizzi, *Progressive and Underground Music '67 – '76* (Giunti Editore, Florence, Italy, 2003).

Will Romano, *Mountains Come Out of the Sky: The Illustrated History of Prog Rock*, (Backbeat Books, Milwaukee, WI, USA, 2010). Foreword by Bill Bruford.

Will Romano, *Prog Rock FAQ: All That's Left to Know about Rock's Most Progressive Music* (Backbeat Books, Milwaukee, WI, USA, 2015).

Alex Ross, *Listen to This* (Fourth Estate, New York, NY, USA, 2010).

Alex Ross, *The Rest is Noise: Listening to the Twentieth Century* (Picador, New York, NY, USA, 2007).

Oliver Sacks, *Musicophilia: Tales of Music and the Brain* (Picador, New York, NY, USA, 2011).

Edward W. Said, *Music at the Limits: Three Decades of Essays and Articles on Music* (Bloomsbury, London, UK 2008).

John Schaefer, *New Sounds: A Listener's Guide to New Music* (Harper & Row, New York, NY, USA, 1987).

Charles Snider, *The Strawberry Bricks Guide to Progressive Rock: Revised and Expanded Edition* (strawberrybrick.com, Chicago, IL, USA, second edition 2017).

Anthony Storr, *Music and the Mind* (HarperCollins, New York, NY, USA, 1997).

Paul Stump, *The Music's All That Matters: A History of Progressive Rock* (Quartet Book, London, UK, 1997).

Michael Tippett, ed. Meirion Bowen, *Music of the Angels: Essays and Sketchbooks of Michael Tippett* (Eulenberg Books, 1980).

Paul Trynka, *The Electric Guitar* (Virgin Books, London, UK, 1993).

David Weigel, *The Show That Never Ends: The Rise and Fall of Prog Rock* (W. W. Norton and Co, New York, NY, USA, 2017).

Victoria Williamson, *You Are the Music: How Music Reveals What it Means to be Human* (Icon Books, London, UK, 2015).

Appendix III: Yes Classics

Rather than list every track on every album, I have taken the risky decision to list the material from Yes's recorded history – 75 tracks in all – which I would personally include in a definitive 'best of' compilation. This would be my own take, in other words, on a 'Yes canon' for the future. The reader is free to, and almost certainly will, disagree. I set myself the aim of including at least one track from all 21 (22 if you recognise both *Keys to Ascension* studio and live compilations), and found it relatively natural to do so. I included the compilation *Yesterdays* in this album list, as that is the only way of including 'America'. Though I hold a particular regard for the 1971–1977 period, as will become evident, I appreciate and enjoy Yes music across the whole span of their career. Omission of a track here does not imply that I dislike it, simply that I don't regard it as essential in relaying what Yes is and will be across the decades. Not does inclusion here imply equivalence with other material. But taken as a whole, I would see this as a good reflection of the best of Yes. I confess that I might not have included 'Owner' on my list, but for the fact that the song – which is a very well crafted slice of arty pop – is so permanently identified with the band. There will be other surprise omissions and inclusions here, for sure. The finale to Stravinsky's 'Firebird Suite' and to Britten's 'The Young Person's Guide to the Orchestra' are the most regular opening pieces for a Yes concert down the years, and deserve to be added to this list for that reason.

Yes (Atlantic Records, 1969)
- Beyond and Before
- I See You

Time and a Word (Atlantic Records, 1970)
- Everydays
- The Prophet
- Astral Traveller

The Yes Album (Atlantic Records, 1971)
- Yours Is No Disgrace
- Clap
- Starship Trooper
- I've Seen All Good People
- A Venture
- Perpetual Change

Fragile (Atlantic Records, 1971)
- Roundabout
- South Side of the Sky
- Long Distance Runaround
- The Fish (Schindleria Primaturus)
- Mood For a Day
- Heart of the Sunrise

Close to the Edge (Atlantic Records, 1972)
- Close to the Edge
- And You and I
- Siberian Khatru

216 • Solid Mental Grace: Listening to the Music of Yes

Tales from Topographic Oceans (Atlantic Records, 1973)
- The Revealing Science of God
- The Remembering
- The Ancient
- Ritual: Nous Sommes du Soleil

Relayer (Atlantic Records, 1974)
- The Gates of Delirium
- Sound Chaser
- To Be Over

Yesterdays (Atlantic Records, 1975)
- America

Going for the One (Atlantic Records, 1977)
- Parallels
- Turn of the Century
- Wonderous Stories
- Awaken

Tormato (Atlantic Records, 1978)
- Future Times / Rejoice
- Madrigal
- On the Silent Wings of Freedom

Drama (Atlantic Records, 1980)
- Machine Messiah
- Into the Lens
- Tempus Fugit

90125 (Atco, 1983)
- Owner of a Lonely Heart
- Changes
- Cinema
- Hearts

Big Generator (Atco, 1987)
- Rhythm of Love
- Shoot High, Aim Low
- Almost Like Love
- I'm Running

Anderson, Bruford Wakeman, Howe (Arista, 1989) *
- Themes
- Fist of Fire

- Birthright

Union (Arista, 1991)
- Masquerade
- Miracle of Life
- Silent Talking
- The More We Live – Let Go

Talk (Victory Music, 1994)
- Real Love
- Where Will You Be?
- Endless Dream

Keys to Ascension (Essential, 1996)
- That, That Is

Keys to Ascension 2 (Essential, 1997)
- Mind Drive
- Children of Light

Open Your Eyes (Eagle Records, 1997)
- New State of Mind
- Universal Garden
- Fortune Seller
- The Solution

The Ladder (Eagle Records, 1999)
- It Will Be A Good Day
- New Language
- Nine Voices

Magnification (Eagle Records, 2001)
- Spirit of Survival
- Can You Imagine
- Dreamtime
- In the Presence Of

Fly From Here (Frontiers, 2011)
- Fly From Here
- Solitaire
- Into the Storm

Heaven & Earth (Frontiers, 2014)
- Light of the Ages
- Subway Walls

Appendix IV: Further Resources

In addition to books, recorded music and DVDs (both official and unofficial) there is a vast quantity of material about Yes across the Internet. The official band site can be found at http://yesworld.com, and the official Yes mailing list can be subscribed to at http://eepurl.com/zMol9. On Facebook see: https://www.facebook.com/yestheband/. On Twitter: @yesofficial. Individual band member sites and other sources are linked from 'YesWorld'.

The original Yes Internet source, *Notes From the Edge*, an interactive and interview-based magazine, has moved from emailing list to the web and now to Facebook at: https://www.facebook.com/NotesFromtheEdge. The Wikipedia page on Yes has also benefitted from a number of expert contributors over the years, and provides a decent overview of the band: https://en.wikipedia.org/wiki/Yes_(band)

Regular, reliable, referenced and sourced news about the band, its members and offshoots (including touring, recording, related media, announcements and projects) can be found at 'Where Are They Now? – Yes', updated regularly by Henry Potts: http://www.bondegezou.co.uk/wnyesm.htm. Along with Matt Putzel, Henry also runs the wide-ranging 'Yescography' site: http://www.relayer35.com/Yescography/home.htm.

'Yes Music Podcast', hosted by Kevin Mulryne and Mark Anthony K, is a free, extensive, weekly show which has been appearing since August 2011 and is archived online: https://yesmusicpodcast.com/about/. Miguel Falcão (miguelbass on YouTube) has produced some fine, technically highly skilled covers of Chris Squire's bass compositions, along with some good transcriptions. Other transcriptions are listed in Appendix II.

The most comprehensive account of Yes's concert career can be found on 'Forgotten Yesterdays', which features dates and venues, setlists, reviews (including a number by the author of this book), photos, video and recording links, tour programme reproductions, memorabilia and more. Established in 1996, it is a curated, fan-generated site run by Steven Sullivan and Pete Whipple at: http://forgotten-yesterdays.com/ See also Steve's 'Yesgigs 1966–1980': http://www.m-ideas.com/sullivan/Yesgigs.html. The widest range of unlicensed live recordings of Yes concerts from the earliest years, including some rarities and demos, can be found at Remy Menting's 'Songs of the Earth': http://www.yessongs.nl. Related material can be discovered at Lee's fascinating 'Yes Museum', established in 1995: http://yesmuseum.org.

In terms of online discussion forums, the original UseNet group was alt. music.yes, established in June 1994 (and which this author was active in from 1996 to 2003). It is now a virtually disused Google Group. The major forum these days, one that has been running for over 15 years with some 10,000 members and several hundred fairly regular participants, is Tim Lutterbie's 'YesFans': http://www.yesfans.com/ (where the author may also be found occasionally since 2004). There are numerous sites and forums across the world, including, for example, the Scottish Yes Network (https://www.facebook.com/pg/Chris-Squires-Scottish-Yes-Network), YesFocus in the Netherlands (www.yesfocus.eu/yesfocus.eu/) and YesFanz (Brian Draper) in Australia and New Zealand.

In relation to print fanzines, there have been many over the years, until they were largely superseded by the web. *Yes Fanzine*, founded in 2012, is still going, featuring original photos and artwork. Three high-quality print issues are available from http://www.awakeningcomics.webs.com and https://www.facebook.com/YesFanzine/.

Probably the best known fanzine from the recent past was the semi-official and lavishly produced *Yes Magazine*, edited in the US by Doug and Glenn Gottlieb, who went on to produce official tour programmes, are co-ordinating the official Yes 50th Anniversary photo project, and can now be found at: https://gottliebbros.com/. Also worth mentioning is Suzanne Cerquone and Christine Holz's *Wonderous Stories* (USA), *Sound Chaser* (Barry Smith) from the early 1980s, *Relayer* (USA, thirty issues, Tanya Coad and Sue Jones), *Relayer* (UK, twelve issues in the 1980s), *Close to Yes* (Belgium, 1985–1992), *Topographic Sounds* (Spain, 1990–1994, four issues) *Yes Family Fan Club* (Japan, in Japanese), and two UK-based magazines this author contributed to over the years: *Yes Music Circle* and cognates, edited by Tiz Hay, and *The Revealing*, edited by Paul Williams and Ian Hartley, both published in the late 1980s through to the 1990s.

In terms of what gets labelled 'progressive rock' more broadly, see *Prog* magazine (http://teamrock.com/prog), the leading regular UK publication in this area of music; *Progression* (http://www.progressionmagazine.com), the journal of progressive music in the USA; the music, production and commentary of Steven Wilson (http://stevenwilsonhq.com/sw/); Burning Shed (https://burningshed.com), an independent record label established in April 2001 by musicians Tim Bowness and Pete Morgan, and Digital Global Mobile (https://www.dgmlive.com), an independent record label founded in 1992 by Robert Fripp and producer/online content developer David Singleton. *The Wire* is essential reading for all things avant and outré. MoonJune Records (https://moonjunerecords.bandcamp.com) explore the boundaries of progressive music with jazz, rock, ethno and experimental.

Cultured Llama Publishing
Poems | Stories | Curious Things

Cultured Llama was born in a converted stable. This creature of humble birth drank greedily from the creative source of the poets, writers, artists and musicians that visited, and soon the llama fulfilled the destiny of its given name.

Cultured Llama aspires to quality from the first creative thought through to the finished product.

www.culturedllama.co.uk

Also published by Cultured Llama

Curious things

Digging Up Paradise: Potatoes, People and Poetry in the Garden of England by Sarah Salway
Paperback; 164pp; 203×203mm; 76 colour illus.; 978-0-9926485-6-5; June 2014

Punk Rock People Management: A No-Nonsense Guide to Hiring, Inspiring and Firing Staff by Peter Cook
Paperback; 40pp; 210×148mm; 978-0-9932119-0-4; February 2015

Do it Yourself: A History of Music in Medway by Stephen H. Morris
Paperback; 504pp; 229×152mm; 978-0-9926485-2-7; April 2015

The Music of Business: Business Excellence Fused with Music by Peter Cook
Paperback; 318pp; 210×148mm; 978-0-9932119-1-1; May 2015

The Hungry Writer by Lynne Rees
Paperback; 246pp; 244×170mm; 57 colour illus.; 978-0-9932119-3-5; September 2015

Short stories

Canterbury Tales on a Cockcrow Morning by Maggie Harris
Paperback; 138pp; 203×127mm; 978-0-9568921-6-4; September 2012

As Long as it Takes by Maria C. McCarthy
Paperback; 168pp; 203×127mm; 978-0-9926485-1-0; February 2014

In Margate by Lunchtime by Maggie Harris
Paperback; 204pp; 203×127mm; 978-0-9926485-3-4; February 2015

The Lost of Syros by Emma Timpany
Paperback; 128pp; 203×127mm; 978-0-9932119-2-8; July 2015

Only the Visible Can Vanish by Anna Maconochie
Paperback; 158pp; 203×127mm; 978-0-9932119-9-7; September 2016

Who Killed Emil Kreisler? by Nigel Jarrett
Paperback; 208pp; 203×127mm; 978-0-9568921-1-9; November 2016

A Short History of Synchronised Breathing and other stories by Vanessa Gebbie
Paperback; 132pp; 203×127mm; 978-0-9568921-2-6; February 2017

In the Wild Wood by Frances Gapper
Paperback; 212pp; 203×127mm; 978-0-9957381-6-4; June 2017

A Witness of Waxwings by Alison Lock
Paperback; 128pp; 203×127mm; 978-0-9957381-5-7; December 2017

Poetry

strange fruits by Maria C. McCarthy
Paperback; 72pp; 203×127mm; 978-0-9568921-0-2; July 2011

A Radiance by Bethany W. Pope
Paperback; 72pp; 203×127mm; 978-0-9568921-3-3; June 2012

The Night My Sister Went to Hollywood by Hilda Sheehan
Paperback; 82pp; 203×127mm; 978-0-9568921-8-8; March 2013

Notes from a Bright Field by Rose Cook
Paperback; 104pp; 203×127mm; 978-0-9568921-9-5; July 2013

The Fire in Me Now by Michael Curtis
Paperback; 90pp; 203×127mm; 978-0-9926485-4-1; August 2014

Cold Light of Morning by Julian Colton
Paperback; 90pp; 203×127mm; 978-0-9926485-7-2; March 2015

Zygote Poems by Richard Thomas
Paperback; 66pp; 178×127mm; 978-0-9932119-5-9; July 2015

Les Animots: A Human Bestiary by Gordon Meade, images by Douglas Robertson
Hardback; 166pp; 203×127mm; 70 line illus.; 978-0-9926485-9-6; December 2015

Memorandum: Poems for the Fallen by Vanessa Gebbie
Paperback; 90pp; 203×127mm; 978-0-9932119-4-2; February 2016

The Light Box by Rosie Jackson
Paperback; 108pp; 203×127mm; 978-0-9932119-7-3; March 2016

There Are No Foreign Lands by Mark Holihan
Paperback; 96pp; 203×127mm; 978-0-9932119-8-0; June 2016

After Hours by David Cooke
Paperback; 92pp; 203×127mm; 978-0-9957381-0-2; April 2017

There Are Boats on the Orchard by Maria C. McCarthy
Paperback; 36pp; 210×115mm; SKU: 001; July 2017

Hearth by Rose Cook
Paperback; 120pp; 203×127mm; 978-0-9957381-4-0; September 2017

The Year of the Crab by Gordon Meade
Paperback; 88pp; 203×127mm; 978-0-9957381-3-3; October 2017

Lightning Source UK Ltd.
Milton Keynes UK
UKHW03f1009160318
319567UK00001B/60/P